MAKERS
of the
MUSLIM
WORLD

Fazlallah Astarabadi and The Hurufis

"Shahzad Bashir is to be commended for producing a remarkably accessible work on a complex subject; his explanations are models of lucidity and brevity."

PROFESSOR DEVIN DEWEESE, INDIANA UNIVERSITY

SELECTION OF TITLES IN THE MAKERS OF THE MUSLIM WORLD SERIES

Series editor: Patricia Crone,
Institute for Advanced Study, Princeton

'Abd al-Malik, Chase F. Robinson
Abd al-Rahman III, Maribel Fierro
Abu Nuwas, Philip Kennedy
Ahmad ibn Hanbal, Christopher Melchert
Ahmad Riza Khan Barelwi, Usha Sanyal
Al-Ma'mun, Michael Cooperson
Al-Mutanabbi, Margaret Larkin
Amir Khusraw, Sunil Sharma
El Hajj Beshir Agha, Jane Hathaway
Fazlallah Astarabadi and the Hurufis, Shazad Bashir
Ibn 'Arabi, William C. Chittick
Ibn Fudi, Ahmad Dallal
Ikhwan al-Safa, Godefroid de Callatay
Shaykh Mufid, Tamima Bayhom-Daou

For current information and details of other books in the series, please visit www.oneworld-publications.com/makers-of-the-muslim-world

MAKERS
of the
MUSLIM
WORLD

Fazlallah Astarabadi and The Hurufis

SHAHZAD BASHIR

ONEWORLD
ACADEMIC

FAZLALLAH ASTARABADI AND THE HURUFIS

A Oneworld Book
First published by Oneworld Publications, 2005
Reprinted, 2019

A CIP record for this title is available
from the British Library

ISBN 978-1-85168-385-7
eISBN 978-1-78074-192-5

Typeset by Jayvee, India
Cover and text designed by Design Deluxe
Printed and Bound in Great Britain
by Clays Ltd, Elcograf S.p.A.

Oneworld Publications
10 Bloomsbury Street
London, WC1B 3SR
England

TO MY PARENTS AND GRANDMOTHER

CONTENTS

PREFACE

Fazlallah Astarabadi (d. 1394) was an Islamic religious leader who believed that the world was about to come to an end and that he had been appointed the final divine messenger for humanity. He claimed that he had received direct revelations from God, which made him equal to prophets like Moses, Jesus, and Muhammad. These revelations came to him in the form of momentous dreams that also gave him the unsurpassed ability to interpret others' dreams and to understand all human and animal languages. His followers thought that he was the ultimate master of all techniques of interpretation and, based on this distinction, they saw him as a manifestation of God in a human body.

Divine incarnation is a radical idea in the Islamic context and readers of this book already familiar with Islam might be inclined to think that Fazlallah and his followers do not qualify as Muslims. Such a judgment should be resisted. All evidence from Fazlallah's works indicates that he considered himself a Muslim, but he also felt that he had been given the great charge of fulfilling Muhammad's mission by providing the final and unambiguous interpretation of the Qur'an and previous scriptures. It is understandable that Muslims who did not accept Fazlallah's claims saw him as a transgressor but, from a historical viewpoint, we must regard Fazlallah's story as an indicator of Islam's internal diversity. The radical ideas held by Fazlallah had, by the time of his activity, a long history as a part of the fabric of Islam. He provided a new complicated rationale for the proposition that God can manifest himself in the material world and was able to persuade a sizeable group that his views represented true Islam. His perspective should be seen as a version of Islam that was a viable alternative for Muslims living in the late medieval period.

The first three chapters of this book treat Fazlallah's life and the next two go into aspects of his thought. Chapter 4, on cosmology and humanity, explains Fazlallah's ideas about the creation of the world, its mythological history, and the place of the human being within it. The human body in particular was a central topic for him since he believed that the human form was an actual image of God imprinted on a mixture of earthly elements. He was also especially concerned with the human capacity for language, spoken as well as written. This emphasis is reflected in the fact that his followers came to be known as "Hurufis," a term that translates as "letterists" and implies people obsessed with the alphabet. As discussed in Chapter 5, Fazlallah's perspective compelled him and his followers to work for the salvation of the world in the face of the impending apocalypse. This effort generated a substantial literary corpus as well as communities of followers in various parts of the Iranian world. Chapter 6 takes the narrative beyond Fazlallah's death by treating the activities of his immediate followers who constructed a shrine for him after his execution and attempted to rationalize his death. The last chapter of the book describes the fate of Fazlallah's ideas after the period of his direct disciples.

Although written for a non-specialist audience, this book is the most comprehensive academic treatment of Fazlallah Astarabadi and his movement to date. A National Endowment for the Humanities Fellowship from the American Research Institute in Turkey was instrumental in providing the resources for manuscript research for this project. I am grateful to Patricia Crone, for her keen editorial eye, and to Hamid Algar,

Abbas Amanat, Kathryn Babayan, Gerhard Böwering, Kay Ebel Cornell Fleischer, Adnan Husain, Ahmet Karamustafa, and Emin Lelic for their aid and encouragement over the years I have been pursuing this topic. Special thanks to members of the Sufis and Society Project – Devin DeWeese, Jamal Elias, Farooq Hamid, Kishwar Rizvi, and Sara Wolper – for providing a congenial venue for discussing many different interests. And my greatest gratitude is due to Nancy and Zakriya for all their patience and love.

1

EARLY LIFE

Very little is known for certain about Fazlallah Astarabadi's life. He is mentioned in only two historical works, which state that his birth name was 'Abd al-Rahman, but he was better known as Abu l-Fazl Astarabadi, or as Sayyid Fazlallah. At some point in his life, he acquired a considerable reputation for a religious lifestyle emphasizing poverty and detachment from the world and for the depth and literary quality of his writings. Muslim scholars in Samarqand (Central Asia) and Gilan (northern Iran) eventually condemned his views as religious innovation, a hallmark of heresy in medieval Islamic thought. The historians state that he was executed on the order of the Turko-Mongol conqueror Timur in the Islamic year 804 (1401–2 CE). The involvement of Timur in the matter is certain, though it can be asserted, on the basis of better evidence, that the execution actually took place in 1394.

The lack of hard historical information does not mean that nothing else can be said about Fazlallah's life. His followers' works provide many details, some even with dates, although these sources have to be treated with caution since they presume that Fazlallah was a great saint and a martyr. Whatever is said in these works comes to us after being refracted through the lens of the myth Fazlallah's followers built around his personality during his life and after his death. This issue is further complicated by the fact that Fazlallah and his followers placed great importance on dreams. Much of what we know about his life consists of either his own dreams and their supposed meanings, or the interpretation he provided for dreams seen by others. Such information is often difficult to interpret conclusively, leading to a story full of conjectures.

My sketch of Fazlallah's life is based largely on the movement's internal tradition. Its neat progression, where everything works out like a plan, makes it difficult to accept the whole narrative as history on face value. Since we have virtually no evidence from outside the movement, we cannot make the story more complex by juxtaposing alternative information and interpretations, as would be done with an historical topic based on a wider base of sources. We have to take the story as it is, keeping in mind that it is both a history and the unfolding of a myth or an archetype. Fazlallah's devoted followers must have witnessed their guide's life as a complex reality as well. The fact that what they recorded from it seems formulaic and oversimplified reflects their notions of the light in which Fazlallah's life should be understood. In what follows, I reconstruct Fazlallah's life using the fragmentary evidence found in his own works and the eulogistic accounts written by his followers.

BIRTH AND CHILDHOOD

Works by Fazlallah's followers tell us that he was born in Astarabad in 1340. The city, the capital of an Iranian province on the southeastern shore of the Caspian Sea (see map), was at the time under the control of a petty ruler from the Ilkhan dynasty. Fazlallah's father was the head judge of the city, which placed his family among the local elite. The fact that the term "sayyid" is sometimes attached to Fazlallah's name means that he considered himself a descendant of Muhammad, a mark of distinction among Muslims. The city of Astarabad was, at least in later centuries, famous for having a large number of sayyids as its residents, which made some people regard it as a religious center. We do not know to which sect of Islam Fazlallah's family belonged. His works reflect familiarity with the positions of various sects but also show a particular devotion to early leaders of Twelver Shi'ism known as the imams. However, a report from one of his sons that originated after Fazlallah's death states that the family was Sunni of the Shafi'i legal persuasion. The confusion regarding this matter in part reflects the fact that formal sectarian affiliation was not a crucial marker of religious identity in the context.

Fazlallah's father died while he was still a child and we are told that he inherited the judge's office. Judgeships were not usually transferable between generations and if Fazlallah did actually succeed his father in this way, this would have been based on a limited local tradition. In his youth, while he was incapable of actually doing the judge's job, he was put on a horse every day and taken to the courthouse to act as the figurehead while his father's former assistants took care of the work. The judge's seat he occupied may have made him unusually serious even as a child, but we are also told that he was naturally inclined toward religious diligence. He performed the necessary Islamic rituals without fail from an early age and often went beyond these to do extra prayers by staying awake at night. He must have received a solid traditional religious education in his youth as well since his works, written much later in his life, show extensive familiarity with major Islamic sources, such as the Qur'an and the sayings of Muhammad and other early Muslims. The interpretive method he eventually developed also contains ways of arguing that he could have learned only through training in a traditional institution.

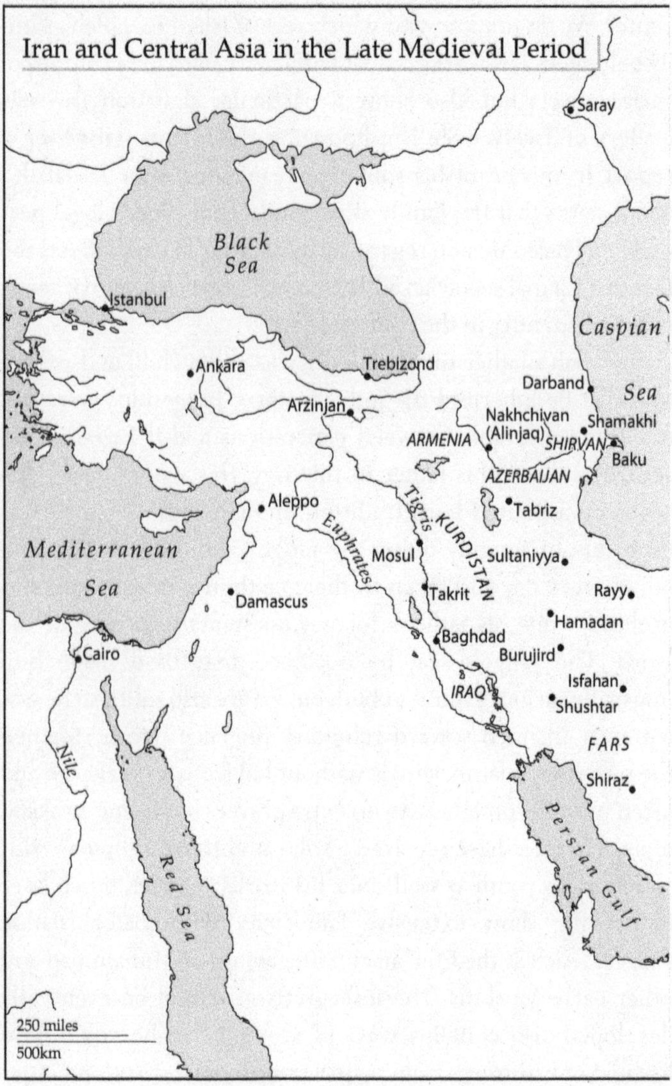
Iran and Central Asia in the Late Medieval Period
Saray
Black Sea
Istanbul
Caspian Sea
Ankara
Trebizond
Darband
Arzinjan
Nakhchivan (Alinjaq)
Shamakhi
ARMENIA
SHIRVAN
Baku
AZERBAIJAN
Aleppo
Tabriz
Tigris
KURDISTAN
Euphrates
Mediterranean Sea
Mosul
Sultaniyya
Takrit
Rayy
Damascus
Hamadan
Baghdad
Cairo
Burujird
Isfahan
IRAQ
Shushtar
FARS
Nile
Shiraz
Persian Gulf
Red Sea
250 miles
500km

Map by MAPgrafix

Fazlallah's first extraordinary religious experience occurred around the year 1358 at the age of eighteen. One day he heard a wandering dervish recite the following verse by the great Sufi Persian poet Jalal al-Din Rumi (d. 1273):

> Why are you afraid of death when you have the essence of eternity?
> How can a grave contain you when you have the light of God?

This verse moved Fazlallah greatly, so much so that he became rooted to the spot and went into a kind of trance. He then asked his religious teacher about the verse's meaning and was told that it was beyond description. He said that understanding the message underlying the verse required devoting oneself completely to religious pursuits, following which one would experience the meaning rather than knowing it intellectually. Hoping to unite with God and transcend death as mentioned in the verse, Fazlallah decided to attempt the experiential path suggested by his teacher.

RELIGIOUS WANDERING

For one whole year after hearing the verse, Fazlallah tried to live a normal life while at the same time detaching himself from worldly concerns. During the day he would go to the religious school to study and also work as a judge as required by the office he had inherited. At night he would often remove himself to a graveyard outside the city and pray alone until dawn. He soon discovered that his day and night-time activities were fundamentally antithetical to each other and that he must make a choice. When he was about nineteen, he decided to abandon his family, possessions, and secure life to become a homeless religious seeker. He gave away all his belongings and left

Astarabad in the dark of the night. On the way out of the city, he met a shepherd and gave him the clothes he was wearing in exchange for a felt shirt. From now on he began wearing this shirt at all times as a symbol of having abandoned worldly connections and comforts.

Fazlallah's religious search first took him to the city of Isfahan in central Iran. He was unused to hard conditions and the long journey on foot from Astarabad caused him to develop a seizure in one of his limbs upon arrival. After recovering, he became a part of the culture of wandering religious seekers who were becoming common in the Islamic world at this time. The period 1300–1500 is known for the rise of groups such as the Haydaris, Qalandars, and Abdals of Rum, whose members demonstrated their religious devotion by shunning contact with the larger society and by deliberately violating codes of conduct relating to clothing, diet, and normative religious practices such as daily prayers. Fazlallah never joined a group especially committed to breaking social norms but had contacts with people who had adopted such an attitude.

In Isfahan, Fazlallah also began to experience significant dreams, which he was able to interpret in correlation with his waking experience. For instance, he saw a disturbing dream in which an uncouth man took him by the hand near a water bank and spun him around three times. A few days later, he ran into a group of men who invited him to come with them to the river. He went with them but then found them not to his liking because of their questionable religious behavior. He had a meal with them, after which they started to dance while he sat by the side hoping not to be asked to join in. However, one of the men came over and made him stand up and spin around three times just as in the dream. Fazlallah's initial unease about the dream was now relieved since he realized that it had been a premonition regarding the future.

After some time in Isfahan, Fazlallah decided to undertake the hajj, the obligatory Muslim pilgrimage to Mecca. His works contain extended commentaries on the significance of the Ka'ba, the cube-like shrine in Mecca that is at the center of the hajj, and we can presume that the pilgrimage was a moment of great significance in his life. After the pilgrimage, he traveled to the city of Khwarazm, south of the Aral Sea in Central Asia, and from there decided to embark once again on a pilgrimage to Mecca. On the way, however, he got caught up in heavy snows in the mountains of Luristan. While waiting for the roads to clear, he saw a dream in which a man told him to change his course and go instead to the city of Mashhad. He soon realized that this man was the ninth Shi'i imam Musa al-Riza (d. 818) who is buried in Mashhad. This city, now in northeastern Iran, has been a major pilgrimage center for Shi'i Muslims in particular since the ninth century. Interpreting the dream as an invitation, Fazlallah went to Mashhad and felt that the religious exercises he performed at the imam's shrine were particularly beneficial for his spiritual progress. He then restarted his journey to Mecca and, after the hajj, decided to travel once again to Khwarazm.

DREAMS IN KHWARAZM

Fazlallah was in his early twenties when he arrived in Khwarazm for the second time. The two dreams mentioned above reflect his developing sense that he had a special aptitude for communication with the unseen sacred world through the medium of sleep. The first dream gave him knowledge of the future, and in the second, a long dead divine made an appearance to guide him in his religious search. The dreams he saw in Khwarazm continued this pattern; he now came into contact with even greater guides and was told things known only to the very elect.

One day in Khwarazm, Fazlallah fell asleep while doing repetitive Sufi prayers, called *zikr*, with the formula "there is no god but God." He then saw that he was in a bathhouse when Jesus came in and asked him if he knew the names of the most sincere religious seekers over the course of Islamic history. He said that he did not know and was then told that these were the four famous Sufis Ibrahim Adham, Bayazid Bistami, Sahl b. 'Abdallah Tustari, and Bahlul. These names remained with him when he awoke and he said that this knowledge allowed him to understand many things. The point of the dream presumably was to indicate that the opinions attributed to these four were to be preferred over other interpretations of early Sufi thought and practice.

A few days later, Fazlallah had a dream in which he was standing next to Solomon. The prophet asked him if such and such a person had been oppressing him. He said yes and then Solomon asked the hoopoe bird, his trusted lieutenant mentioned in the Qur'an (27: 20), to fetch this man. The hoopoe left and came back with a black crow that turned out to be the offending man in a transformed condition. Solomon then scolded the crow severely and eventually asked the hoopoe to kill him.

In a different version of this dream, Fazlallah saw himself in the garden of his former home in Astarabad when a man came in and expelled him from it using harsh language. He then found himself standing as a supplicant in front of Solomon who was seated on a heavenly throne. Solomon called the hoopoe and asked him to bring the other party involved in the dispute so that he could pass a judgment. The hoopoe went and brought back a black crow, and Solomon ordered all the feathers of the crow to be plucked out. The crow was then thrown out of the garden and Fazlallah was made the garden's owner. He later said that he understood the dream as follows: Solomon was God, the garden was Fazlallah's body, the hoopoe his spirit, and the crow the part of the human soul that incites to evil. The dream's message was that Fazlallah's evil self had caused him to become angry when the man had expelled him from the garden in the beginning of the dream. God had then intervened and made Fazlallah's spirit incapacitate the evil self and expel it from his body.

The two versions of this dream contain rather different messages. The first represents the idea of supernatural protection for Fazlallah from his enemies, while the second indicates that the real conflict lay not in his relationships with others but in the battle that was taking place between different aspects of his own psyche. The most plausible explanation for the difference between the two versions is that Fazlallah gave different accounts of the dream to his followers, modifying both the details and the supposed message according to the situation. Whatever accounts for the difference, it is clear that he saw dreams as a major tool for both self-analysis and understanding his relationships with others.

Another dream seen in Khwarazm anticipates the idea that Fazlallah would become the best dream interpreter of all times. This time he saw himself near a tree in Astarabad, under which sat an old soothsayer preparing to furnish interpretations for people's dreams and other concerns. Muhammad appeared and told the old man that what he was about to attempt was a very difficult business since knowing true interpretations required being able to establish the correct connections between one's own self, the dreamer, and any other person dead or alive. The persons actually seen in the dreams were not to be taken for their surface identities but were to be understood as stand-ins for others. Knowing who each character really was required a comprehensive understanding that went far beyond the dream that was the immediate concern.

After saying this, Muhammad turned to Fazlallah and said that the gift of true dream interpretation is like a rare star that becomes visible every thirty thousand years and encompasses seventy thousand worlds. He then told Fazlallah that this star had now appeared and he could see it if he wished. He was told to go and stand under an orange tree where he would see seven stars, one of them being bigger and more luminous than the others. He did so and the luminous star emitted a ray of light that entered his right eye, conveying a special intuitive knowledge to him. He said that the ray of light felt like a pearly substance, which disclosed to him secret meanings of Muhammad's sayings (hadith). In one report about the dream, he said that the light kept flowing until the whole star had poured into his eye. When he woke up from this dream he felt that he could intuitively interpret all dreams and could also understand the language of birds.

The powers revealed in the dream of the star seen in Khwarazm remained Fazlallah's greatest religious claim through the rest of his life. His followers called him the master of esoteric interpretation (*sahib-i ta'vil*) because they thought that he could penetrate the surfaces of all events and narratives to figure out their true meanings. Dreams and the language of birds do not hold obvious meanings for human beings but Fazlallah felt that God had made him capable of translating such things into intelligible matters. He had received his knowledge in stages, through the intermediacy of guides such as the imam Musa al-Riza and the prophets Jesus, Solomon, and Muhammad who had appeared to him in his dreams.

The story of Fazlallah's alleged interpretive powers spread rapidly throughout Khwarazm and he began to be surrounded by people seeking explanations for their own stories. However, he preferred to keep the company of individuals who exercised control over themselves through perpetual silence and fasting and were dedicated to religious pursuits alone. The crowd around him kept growing so that he eventually decided to leave Khwarazm altogether.

SABZAVAR

We can place Fazlallah in the region of Sabzavar, in northeastern Iran, within the earliest period of his activity after the dreams seen in Khwarazm. This is significant because a substantial proportion of the local population in Sabzavar was involved in apocalyptic religious activity at this time. During the period 1336–1381, this region was under the rule of a group of nobility called the Sarbadars. The Sabzavar state was quite unique in that, unlike the governments of all other surrounding regions, the Sarbadars did not follow a dynastic principle. They themselves were a diverse collection of noble families with competing interests and claims. The families sometimes supported each other against other groups, but at other times, the group disintegrated owing to bitter infighting. The region's tradesmen's guilds (particularly the butchers and the undertakers) wielded considerable power in the state and a butcher in fact became the ruler for a brief period around 1356.

Adding to the complexity of the social environment, a substantial proportion of the population of Sabzavar was affiliated with a religious group called the Shaykhiyya that was led by a series of charismatic religious guides between 1330 and 1380. These religious leaders – Shaykh Khalifa (d. 1335), Shaykh Hasan Juri (d. 1342), Darvish 'Aziz Muhammadi (d. 1362–63), and Darvish Rukn al-Din (d. 1380–81) – had political ambitions and each of them was killed in the course of factional fighting between the interest groups within the state. The details of the religious views held by the Shaykhiyya are not fully known but it is clear that, at least at times, the leaders advised their followers to prepare arms in advance of a great cosmic war that would be followed by the appearance of the messiah. The immediacy of the expectation can be seen in the report that for a number of years, a horse was placed at the gates of the city of Sabzavar every day to become the messiah's steed when he made his appearance.

Fazlallah's presence in an area with a high messianic expectation may have been tied to his growing sense of his own significance. He could have gone to Sabzavar in the light of his expanding repertoire of extraordinary experiences and may have absorbed the apocalyptic currents that were in the air in Sabzavar at the time into his own ideas. We cannot be sure of this, but it would make sense that living in a population expecting a messiah eventually compelled Fazlallah to think of himself in such terms.

Stories about Fazlallah's activity in Sabzavar do not state that he portrayed himself as the messiah. Instead, he seems to have acted as a mediator in the state's power politics through his dream interpretation. For instance, we are told that a Sarbadar nobleman named Khwaja Jamal al-Din saw in a dream that he and his uncle 'Ali Mu'ayyad, the Sarbadar incumbent who ruled the state for nearly twenty years between 1361–62 and 1381, caught some pigeons and were cooking them when they grew wings and took off. In the continuation of the dream, he saw that he put a candle in the window of a palace and from that numerous other candles became lit. Jamal al-Din asked Fazlallah for an interpretation but he said that it would have to wait. The Shaykhiyya was at this time in competition with the Sarbadars for control over the state and on a later day, an influential member of this religious fraternity was present in Fazlallah's gathering. At this point, Fazlallah related Jamal al-Din's dream to him and told him that it meant that 'Ali Mu'ayyad would at some point expel members of the Shaykhiyya from Sabzavar but that they would stage a return within a year. This spiritual reconnaissance was clearly meant to aid the Shaykhiyya against the Sarbadars. Fazlallah's follower who tells this story states that this is exactly how things came to pass nearly fifteen years after Fazlallah's prediction. Correlating this account with the history of the Sarbadar state, it would seem that Fazlallah was present in Sabzavar around 1360. Fifteen years later, in 1375, the Shaykhi leader Darvish Rukn al-Din was expelled from Sabzavar, to return in triumph within a year. This calculation for Fazlallah's presence in Sabzavar conflicts with the report that he saw the dream of the star, discussed above, in 765/1363–64 when he was still in Khwarazm. Our sources provide too little information to resolve this discrepancy.

The Sarbadars and their rivals figure in other narratives of Fazlallah's dream interpretation as well, indicating that he spent substantial time and energy in this region. However, he eventually left it and traveled first to Yazd and then on to, once again, Isfahan.

THE RISE TO SOCIAL PROMINENCE

Fazlallah's hagiographers indicate that his decision to leave first Khwarazm and later Sabzavar and Yazd stemmed from his desire to minimize social contact. This idea cannot be accepted at face value. He arrived in Isfahan around 1365 when the city was a bigger and more cosmopolitan urban center than all the cities he had inhabited previously. For someone seeking anonymity, going to a major administrative and commercial center like Isfahan does not make sense. Also, his subsequent behavior in the city gives no indication that he meant to disappear in the crowds of a big city. The move was very likely spurred by the social significance he had acquired in Khwarazm and Sabzavar and represented his desire for increased social exposure rather than an impulse toward isolation.

In Isfahan, Fazlallah made his home in a mosque in the suburb of Tuqchi. Either his fame preceded him or he caught the people's imagination very quickly so that his residence soon became a thoroughfare. Two types of people in particular sought him out: first, dedicated religious seekers searching for a worthy guide, and second, those who wanted him to interpret their dreams. These two groups had interests at cross-purposes with each other and Fazlallah seems to have tried to strike a balance. He was willing to interpret the dreams of anyone who came to see him but made sure that, to preserve his reputation and strict lifestyle, he and his close followers would not receive anything in return. He also continued with austerities such as depriving himself of sleep at night to pray and weep continually in an effort fully to control his carnal desires.

The first person to become attached to him in Isfahan was a Sufi named Mu'in al-Din Shahrastani who questioned him about his understanding of a true "man of God." He replied that he believed in the description given by the famous early Sufi Junayd Baghdadi, who said that it is someone who is silent on the outside so that his inner reality can speak through him. Shahrastani was impressed enough by this answer to become a devotee and after him a number of others also decided to dedicate themselves to Fazlallah. His earliest devotees included Nasrallah Nafaji, whose work *The Book of Dreams* (*Khwabnama*) is one of our main sources for Fazlallah's biography. Imitating the pattern of Fazlallah's own life, his wealthy followers gave away all their belongings to come and live with him in the simple mosque in Tuqchi.

Fazlallah's sincere companions were rewarded for their devotion in the form of spiritual gifts of minor miracles known as *karamat* among Sufis. These included the ability to understand hidden matters, special knowledge pertaining to sacred texts like the Qur'an and the Bible, and clear interpretations of sayings by Muhammad, 'Ali, and other early Islamic heroes. The followers' hermitlike lifestyle and the similarity of their spiritual achievements engendered a deep brotherly feeling among them so that they sometimes thought of themselves as a single soul distributed in many bodies. Their association with Fazlallah also made them subjects of good dreams, whether seen by themselves or those that others saw in which they made appearances.

In contrast with Fazlallah's dedicated devotees, those who came to him seeking interpretations of their dreams included members of the elite such as scholars, sayyids, ministers, military and administrative officers, and wealthy people of all types. They related all manner of dreams in Fazlallah's company and in his response, Fazlallah usually first identified how the dream connected to the dreamers' lives and then gave them information about what was to come. Fazlallah's ability to know the past and predict the future through dreams made him a powerful person. With this information, he was in a position to withhold or disclose secrets and to enable a person to prepare for the future.

Some examples of Fazlallah's dream interpretations are helpful in portraying his life in Isfahan at this point. We are told that a prominent scholar named Sadr al-Din Turka saw a dream in which he was pouring water over Muhammad's hands to help him with the ablutions necessary before ritual prayer. As he bent forward, a drop of his saliva fell from his mouth onto

Muhammad's hands, and this made the prophet look up at him and smile. Fazlallah told Sadr al-Din that the dream indicated that he had been planning to travel to Mecca and stay at the holy sanctuary to write a book harmonizing the principles of divine law and philosophy. His pouring the water represented the idea of writing a book but the intrusion of an impurity in the form of saliva meant that the topic was problematic. Muhammad's looking up and smiling conveyed that, in his view, the divine law revealed to him was too superior a system from philosophy to be compared with it. Sadr al-Din said that he had indeed resolved to write such a book but had not told anyone. The revelation of Muhammad's opinion about the endeavor dissuaded him from beginning the project, and he was saved from doing something objectionable thanks to Fazlallah's interpretation.

Mawlana Zayn al-Din Rajayi was a devoted lay follower of Fazlallah and came one day to tell him a dream in secret. All that was known to others was that the dream had something to do with a slave girl who worked inside his house. Fazlallah told him that the dream revealed that the slave girl was pregnant by him, which the dreamer confirmed. He then predicted that the newborn would be a girl and that, a few days after the birth, he would become very sick and would be delirious for a while. In the end he would be cured and then come and report his experiences to Fazlallah's company. As predicted, a girl was born after two months, and one month later Zayn al-Din became sick and for seven days lost all movement in his body save his breath. He then recovered and the first thing his sight encountered upon gaining consciousness was his new daughter. The story of this dream and Fazlallah's interpretation became very famous and Zayn al-Din would himself tell people about it at length until his death.

Fazlallah's interpretations also include stories in which the occurrences of dreams seem to have no easy symbolic relationship with his interpretation. For example, a military commander named Amir Farrukh Gunbadi saw himself confronted with four dragons. This was interpreted as a reference to a ring of gold and precious stones that the Amir had lost four years ago but would recover in fourteen days. The Amir reported that, exactly according to prediction, he was going through the bazaar two weeks later and paused at the jeweler's shop for a brief moment. Just then another man stopped by and pulled out the ring in an effort to sell it to the jeweler. He recognized the ring and was able to recover it from the man.

The dreams described here show Fazlallah dealing with powerful men such as a famous scholar and a military commander. The fact that people of this stature came to him and told him matters that could reveal the details of their personal lives indicates that they saw him as a trustworthy person. The dreams Fazlallah is reported to have interpreted in Isfahan do not fit any pattern. There are no subjects that receive excessive emphasis, implying that he was acting as a general provider of interpretations to whom anyone could go for a service. His personal ambitions and spiritual life seem to have been on a track that ran parallel to the public persona, the two being relatively independent from each other. We are told that his activities in Isfahan made him famous throughout the provinces of Khurasan, Persian Iraq, Azerbaijan, and Shirvan. The fact that he now decided to leave Isfahan for Tabriz points to his ambition to capitalize on his fame and make a bid for wider influence.

2

ENLIGHTENMENT

Calculating from the few dates at our disposal, Fazlallah arrived in Tabriz some time between 1370 and 1374. The last date for his presence in Isfahan is indicated by the report that he interpreted a dream seen by one of his followers in 772/1370–71, while it is claimed that the Jalayirid ruler Shaykh Uvays, who died in 1374, visited him in Tabriz. This also means that he spent between five and ten years in total in Sabzavar and Isfahan, since the dream of the star, which he saw in Khwarazm, occurred in 765/1363–64.

The city of Tabriz, today the capital of Iran's Azerbaijan province, played a central role in the administration of Iranian lands between the thirteenth and fifteenth centuries. The Mongol conqueror Hülegü (d. 1265), who initiated the Ilkhan dynasty, set up his capital in Maragha, also in Azerbaijan, after his destruction of Baghdad in 1258. The capital was moved to Tabriz in 1265, during the reign of the Ilkhan Abaqa (d. 1282), Hülegü's successor. It was shifted once again in 1313 to the newly constructed Sultaniyya, though Tabriz remained a major commercial and cultural center for the rest of the Ilkhanid period. The Chupanids and the Jalayirids, who supplanted the Ilkhanids in Azerbaijan in rapid succession after the death of the Ilkhan Abu Sa'id in 1335, ruled from Tabriz and regarded control over it as a major source for their political legitimacy.

Although these dynasties ruled only a part of Iran, and that too under highly contentious political circumstances, Tabriz in their times still had the prestige of having been the capital of a grand empire in recent memory. In the fourteenth century, the city's status also rested on the extensive patronage of religion, literature, and art by all the dynasties.

Fazlallah arrived in Tabriz during the twilight years of the reign of Shaykh Uvays, the most significant monarch of the Jalayir dynasty. He made his home in a Sufi hospice and soon became an object of curiosity and devotion among the city's high society. If Shaykh Uvays did himself visit Fazlallah's sessions as reported, he must have acquired a very high status quite quickly indeed. The legendary works on Fazlallah's life also contain references to many other princes, administrators, and military commanders in Tabriz whose dreams Fazlallah is shown to have interpreted effectively. Standard histories of the reign of the Jalayirids in Tabriz make no mention of Fazlallah, casting some doubt on his direct access to the royal court. Although we cannot be sure of the extent of Fazlallah's influence, it is reasonable to assume that he did have some success as an adviser to the elite in Tabriz in the 1370s.

MARRIAGE

Along with associating with rulers and ministers, Fazlallah continued his life of strict asceticism and self-denial in Tabriz. These divergent aspects of his behavior are reflected in the account of his marriage to a woman from the city's nobility. The story indicates that his piety had begun to garner him access to circles of power but that he was keen to maintain his austere lifestyle despite the new connection to the world of privileged classes. Fazlallah's followers included a Jalayir vizier named

Khwaja Bayazid Damghani whose wife, also a devotee, was originally from Astarabad and was related to Fazlallah. This couple wished to arrange the marriage of their fourteen-year-old daughter to Fazlallah but were unsure whether it would be possible. The girl's mother approached Fazlallah through the intermediacy of one of his disciples and was told that the matter was difficult since the circumstances in which Fazlallah lived, which were incumbent on anyone attached to him, would be particularly arduous for a woman. She persisted by asking to hear the exact conditions and was told that the girl would be required to: forsake all personal belongings upon leaving her parents' house; renounce any food or dress that could not be paid for by the small means of a dervish; determine never to take a single step out of the Sufi hospice where Fazlallah lived after entering it; adopt a bed made of sackcloth, a felt pillow, and a cotton dress; respect the religious community's practice of seclusion at night; and adopt the stringent collective prayers practiced daily by the community.

The prospective wife's mother was allegedly glad to hear these conditions and asked the girl what she thought of them. Needless to say, she wholeheartedly agreed due to the spiritual reward she and her parents would attain in return for the harsh life she would lead. She first spent four months in the house of another dervish in a kind of trial to make sure that she could withstand the difficulties and then married Fazlallah. Her entry to the dervish community was marked by the symbolic step of putting on the distinctive green dress worn by all of Fazlallah's dedicated followers. Besides the generally hard living conditions, she also worked alongside other dervishes to sew caps that were sold to provide for the community's food and other bare necessities. In connection with this marriage, Fazlallah was asked about the permissibility of sexual relations and said that they were not spiritually harmful as long as the intention was procreation and not pleasure.

Fazlallah's agreeing to the marriage proposal in Tabriz indicates openness toward establishing ties with elite circles, reflecting his growing connections to matters of politics. Indeed, the discomforts of the ascetic lifestyle would by themselves have been a source of prestige in this society since people considered religious dedication a worthy vocation. His concern with questions of social and political power can be observed in his interpretations of dreams in Tabriz as well. In comparison with the Isfahan period, these stories show that, with time, he had become more aware of the impact of his knowledge on his own and others' interests.

DREAM INTERPRETATION IN TABRIZ

Fazlallah's chief forte in the new city remained dream interpretation, though his behavior seems to have become more of a public performance. We are told that, in his gatherings, he listened to people's accounts and then put his sleeve over his forehead and eyes, in a way removing himself from the company. In the moment of communion with the unseen world, when he discovered the interpretation, the color of his face changed. Then his body returned to normal, and he opened his eyes and stated the interpretation. Occasionally, a dreamer denied what Fazlallah had been able to gather about the dreamer's past, but Fazlallah always stuck to his story as the truth. At other times, Fazlallah actually offered corrections, telling the dreamer that he or she had stated such and such detail incorrectly or had forgotten an important segment. Through such incidents, we get the picture that he had become the dream interpreter par excellence. He seems to have claimed to have completely unfettered access to the whole sphere of consciousness from which dreams emerge.

Fazlallah's increased concern with power is reflected in his interpretations of states and dreams that relate to questions of social status. This included the religious status of those who came to see him and issues having to do with relations between people involving politics. For instance, we are told that he could determine a person's state of ritual purity through dream interpretation or visual observation. Khwaja Hasan Bashtini, a powerful man from the region of Sabzavar, saw that his clothes had caught fire and he had gotten burned. Fazlallah told him that he had had a wet dream the night before but had not noticed it in the morning. He then examined his underwear, saw that this was true, and went to take the bath required after a discharge of semen. Similarly, one of his devoted followers once had a wet dream and decided to just change his clothes and skip the bath. Fazlallah intuited the laxity on the part of the follower as soon as he laid his eyes on him and made a comment that those who wished to have pure hearts should also have clean bodies. The man understood the hint and immediately went to take the bath. Both these incidents mark Fazlallah's own high religious status so that keeping company with him required maintaining particular vigilance with respect to rules of ritual purity.

Stories from Fazlallah's stay in Tabriz have a particular emphasis on questions of sexual impropriety. Fazlallah 'Abidi, an influential citizen in Tabriz, saw a dream in which he was holding a bowl of poison while standing naked. He asked for an interpretation in front of a large group of people and Fazlallah first refused by saying that the matter was not appropriate for discussion. The man insisted so that Fazlallah eventually asked everyone present to leave except for three men who were not from the city. He then told the dreamer that the dream revealed that he had taken a prostitute to his house for two or three nights to satiate his lust and the two lovers had kissed each other's faces. The man refuted this interpretation, upon which Fazlallah related the details of the woman's features and attire. He still refused to acknowledge the incident but then Fazlallah asked one of the others present to validate the interpretation by visiting the prostitute who lived at such and such exact address. When the man stood up to go, Fazlallah 'Abidi asked him to sit back down and acknowledged that the interpretation had been correct.

Fazlallah's alleged ability to know matters relating to sexual impropriety gave him direct power over others since disseminating such information to the public could lead to humiliation, and worse, for the culprits. The most extreme such case is the story of a cloth-seller who opposed Fazlallah and, at one point, went out of his way to call Fazlallah's followers religious deviants. He saw a dream in which he defiled the prayer niche of a mosque and was disturbed enough by it to try Fazlallah for an interpretation. Fazlallah told him that the dream indicated that he had committed incest with his daughter one day when the two were alone in his house. The man became utterly ashamed when told this and asked Fazlallah if there was any way in which he could atone for the sin. Fazlallah replied that the only thing to do was to take a vow never to tell a lie. He replied that it was impossible to be a trader in the bazaar without lying and was then told that none of his words of repentance carried any weight since he was unwilling to stop lying. He became so overwrought with shame when the incident became widely known that he left his established life and moved away from the city. Besides showing Fazlallah's interpretive powers, this story marks Fazlallah's victory over a critic. Its end is predictable given that the source is one of Fazlallah's followers, but we can deduce from it that not everyone was enamored with him during his stay in Tabriz.

A story that shows Fazlallah as a mediator in politics relates to the year 1375 when Shah Shuja' (d. 1384), the Muzaffarid ruler of Shiraz, had ousted the Jalayirids from Tabriz for a very brief period. A scholar named 'Izz al-Din saw a dream in which he traveled somewhere and came across Muhammad sitting down on the ground. He greeted the prophet and the latter raised his hand in front of his face to the level of his eyes with all five fingers spread out. Fazlallah said that the dream revealed that 'Izz al-Din had recently written a treatise dealing with five questions of Islamic jurisprudence and had first dedicated it to Shah Shuja'. But then he had considered the fact that Shah Shuja' was likely to be ousted from Tabriz by the Jalayirids soon and his having dedicated the book to the invader was a risky thing. Consequently, he had removed the dedication from the work's preface. The dreamer confirmed the story and said that Fazlallah's interpretation was miraculous since no one but he himself had known about the book or the inclusion and removal of the dedication.

ENLIGHTENMENT

Fazlallah's personal spiritual development in Tabriz continued, as before, on a path parallel with his public activities. Each dream he was able to interpret both reflected his gift and added to his reserves of knowledge. This process culminated in a special revelation he received in Ramazan 775 (February–March 1374). Nasrallah Nafaji, one of Fazlallah's closest followers, gives the following account of this event:

> During a forty-day retreat in Tabriz, his eminence [i.e. Fazlallah] was favored with a (special) revelation. At this time, spiritual secrets and truths and the stations of Muhammad came within the field of vision of his pure-seeing heart. He now went beyond

> the standing and rank (of others). After the event, he was completely beside himself for three nights and days and wept and lamented uncontrollably. On the third day of this condition, a voice suddenly recited the following verses in his ear:
>
> In the moment he was rent asunder from earthly concerns,
> The world was freed from all calamities.
> (If) someone asks: who is this young man?
> Who is this moon, earth, and heaven?
> It is said: he is the master of the age,
> And the Sultan of all prophets.

The verses enabled Fazlallah to recover from the torment brought on by the revelation. The verses are quite cryptic in the original and the translation above is one among a number of different possible interpretations. What is clear, however, is that they exalted Fazlallah to the level of prophets and beyond, and gave him a pivotal position in the structure of the cosmos. They also emphasized a particular moment in time that correlated his acquiring special knowledge and status with the redemption of the world at large. The idea that he was ranked above all prophets is problematic from a mainstream Islamic viewpoint. The vast majority of Muslims regard prophets as God's most chosen people and see Muhammad as the last prophet and the best of all humans. The status ascribed to Fazlallah in these verses was, therefore, a substantial deviation from what most Muslims alive in Fazlallah's time would have seen as unassailable truths.

The enlightenment experience precipitated a fundamental shift in Fazlallah's view of himself and his purpose in life. A key for appreciating this transformation is the fact that the authors who describe the experience call it a manifestation (*zuhur*) and exteriorization (*buruz*) of God's knowledge and majesty. Since Fazlallah's consciousness and body were the recipients of this manifestation, the event turned him into a sanctified being.

Until this point, his prominence had been based on the following sequence: he heard the concerns of human beings living in the visible world, traveled to the hidden realm to understand them, and came back to tell people what their experiences indicated. After the enlightenment, he no longer needed to travel to the hidden world. Instead, the hidden truths were within him already and his being and activity represented a materialization of the sacred. Those who accepted his claims and tried to reorder their lives according to his commands were thus coming in direct contact with the divine reality.

The reorganization of the flow of knowledge reflected in the enlightenment had significant implications for Fazlallah's actions in the world. The idea that he was equal to prophets meant that his appearance was a direct divine intervention in worldly affairs. His arrival was in some sense preordained and had to fit into the mythological history of the cosmos. This notion tallied neatly with the Islamic expectation of the messiah, the last guide that God is supposed to send to the world before its destruction and the ensuing resurrection. The Islamic messiah is fundamentally an activist figure, charged with dictating the course of history according to the pattern set by God. Therefore, following his identification as the messiah, it no longer sufficed Fazlallah to sit by himself and be a counselor for whoever sought him out. He had to go out into the world and propagate the truths entrusted to him.

ACCEPTING THE MISSION

Our knowledge of the particulars of Fazlallah's activities after the enlightenment remains as murky as that of previous periods. A number of manuscripts containing works by his followers repeat a short list of dates that identifies the year

788/1386–87 as the time of an experience designated the "Manifestation of Divine Glory" (*zuhur-i kibriya*). However, the major enlightenment experience described above, which is also referred to as a form of manifestation (*zuhur*), occurred in 775/1374. The best way to make sense of the two different years marked as moments of grand revelation is to differentiate between the experience itself and its open proclamation. In other words, Fazlallah had the experience of enlightenment in 1374 but he did not proclaim his messianic mission publicly until 1386–87. The period of approximately twelve years between 1374 and 1386 was thus an incubatory phase during which Fazlallah first came to terms with his experience and then gradually conveyed it to his close confidants. The end of the process was an announcement and invitation to the public at large. The fixing of the number of years at twelve may also have been motivated by the desire to emulate the life of the Prophet Muhammad, who preached for twelve years in Mecca, between 610 and 622, before migrating to Yathrib/Medina to set up a separate Muslim community.

Although the precise details of Fazlallah's activity in this period are not known, circumstantial evidence indicates that he spent much time traveling to various areas in the Persian-speaking Islamic world (present-day Iran and Central Asia). The versified *Book of the Divine Footstool* (*Kursinama*) of Fazlallah's major successor 'Ali al-A'la hints that Fazlallah may have tried to abandon all social interaction after the enlightenment. The story is given in cryptic verses and is difficult to make out fully. It suggests that Fazlallah broke off all relationships after the experience of enlightenment and his devotees felt great distress when they were unable to locate him. Finally, 'Ali al-A'la had a dream that led him to a cave where he found Fazlallah living as a hermit. He was unwilling to leave the cave at first but then was told that a dervish nicknamed "traveler" (*musafir*), whom he had known from before, was ill and about to die. As he came to visit this dervish, the latter recognized the station Fazlallah had reached immediately upon seeing his face and greeted him with great enthusiasm. He then correctly told Fazlallah about some of the things he had seen in dreams in Tabriz, proving that the visions were not false but a part of an expectation. He convinced Fazlallah that the knowledge he had been given needed to be conveyed to the whole world. Fazlallah eventually accepted this idea and, reluctantly (we are assured), began his life as a missionary.

Fazlallah's decision to propagate the mission in 1386–87 marked the "Manifestation of Divine Glory" mentioned in numerous works by his followers. While in the initial enlightenment in Tabriz God had manifested himself only to Fazlallah, this was a more momentous occasion since now God was being made available to the larger world through open proclamation of Fazlallah, whom God had chosen as a vessel for himself. Seven close confidants of Fazlallah pledged their allegiance to him at this point, inaugurating a specific group, later called the Hurufis, dedicated to his religious vision. Some of these individuals played a significant part in the later propagation of Fazlallah's message.

POLITICAL AMBITIONS

Fazlallah's surviving works include a short tract entitled *The Book of Sleep* (*Nawmnama*), which provides descriptions of dreams seen between 1383 and 1394. Some of the dreams come with dates and the places where they were seen. From this collection and from works by Fazlallah's followers, we can tell that Fazlallah traveled to various places in Iran, Central Asia, and the Caucasus in the last phase of his life. We now find him in already familiar places such as Isfahan, Tabriz, and Khwarazm, and new localities like Abarquh, Burujird, Damghan, Gilan, Baku, and Shamakhi. These dreams underscore political involvement at three different levels. First, they provide direct evidence for the fact that he saw himself as the messiah, whose mission was ratified by past religious heroes like ʻAli. Second, the dreams indicate that he expected to become a ruler through a political alliance such as marriage to a princess from one of the existing ruling houses. And third, the dreams have a militaristic side, indicating that he thought that he would be installed as a ruler after a bloody struggle.

The narratives given in Fazlallah's *Book of Sleep* are written in a kind of shorthand in the Astarabadi dialect of Persian and it is not always possible to decipher them in full. The idea that he saw himself as the messiah has already been mentioned, and here Fazlallah tells us that, in a dream that occurred in the year 1384, he saw the messiah dressed in white clothes and knew intuitively that these were his clothes. When he awoke he understood that the dream had confirmed that he was the messiah.

In a dream that corroborated the idea that he was heir to the tradition of prophecy, he met ʻAli, who took his hand and said that he swore allegiance to Fazlallah as the leader. This was a reversal of the norm since a figure of ʻAli's status deserves the allegiance of others instead of offering it to someone else. His show of respect to Fazlallah indicated that the latter, as the messiah, now deserved to be respected and followed by all people.

The ambition to be admitted to royal circles is reflected in a dream in which Fazlallah saw Toqtamish Khan (d. 1395), the ruler of the Golden Horde who reigned from the city of Saray in the lower Volga valley (now Russia), and wished that he would get one of his daughters in marriage. He hoped also that the marriage would lead to the birth of a son who would act as a mediator between spiritual and political power represented, respectively, by Fazlallah himself and the royal mother. One of his associates saw a dream seven times, in which a person was identified as "Master of the Auspicious Conjunction" (*sahib-i qiran*), a title referring to an astrological event that marked the astrological charts of rulers. The Master is not identified directly in the dream narrative but it is very likely that it was meant to refer to Fazlallah. He also saw once that drums of happiness were being beaten in Tabriz, as was usually done upon the arrival of a ruler, and realized that he was the object of the celebration.

A number of dreams in the *Book of Sleep* contain imagery of swords that suggests that Fazlallah was contemplating a military role for himself and his followers. One of his followers saw that he had one hundred and forty sons, each equipped with two double-edged swords. Fazlallah also saw that the whole sky was illuminated with a huge sword whose handle he held in his own hand. And in another dream, he saw a sword that had beautiful golden handwriting and stars placed on it in the form of an astronomical chart. He realized that, once again, the handle of the sword was in his hand, and that the text said that the world would experience terrible events after the appearance of Fazlallah Astarabadi.

The dreams from the *Book of Sleep* cited above convey the sense that Fazlallah felt that he was destined to become a ruler as predicted for the Islamic messiah. The allegiance of a grand figure like 'Ali, the possibility of inclusion in an existing royal lineage, and the prospect of a miraculous victory through heavenly weapons as exemplified in the dreams of swords all point in this direction. However, these dreams occur in the work alongside others that have a distinct sense of foreboding. It is almost as if Fazlallah felt that he was definitely destined for something great, but that this would either be a grand victory leading to universal rule, or a horrifying death marking a great cosmic tragedy. For the latter possibility, some of his dreams identify him with Jesus and Husayn, religious figures famous for being subjected to torturous deaths for the sake of their causes. In one dream he even saw that a crippled man had ordered that he was to be captured and imprisoned. This dream is presented as a premonition of the fact that Fazlallah was eventually imprisoned on the order of Timur, famous for being lame. The possibility of martyrdom suggested by these dreams eventually proved truer than Fazlallah's expectation of universal kingship.

3

DEATH

All sources for Fazlallah Astarabadi's life agree that he was executed after a brief imprisonment. However, there is no unanimity over matters such as: what led to this event, when it took place, and what it symbolized. External sources from the fifteenth century and later accounts written by mainstream Muslims portray Fazlallah as a religious extremist who invited the wrath of the rulers owing to his exaggerated claims and political ambition. Among such commentators, some consider the execution justifiable while others offer no moral judgment but present it as a foreseeable consequence of Fazlallah's actions and ideas. Conversely, writings stemming from Fazlallah's movement condemn the execution in the strongest terms. For Fazlallah's followers, the event was a personal shock and a tragedy of cosmic proportions. However, they also felt that Fazlallah's dying in this way was a part of God's cosmic plan and that the tragedy must have an ulterior positive meaning for the future. The fact that the death had to "make sense" in some way meant that Fazlallah's followers had to rethink their religious ideas to a substantial degree after the event.

From a broad historical perspective, Fazlallah's arrest and execution were a side effect of the establishment of the authority of the Turko-Mongol conqueror Timur in Iran and

Central Asia. This region was the scene of massive upheavals during the last quarter of the fourteenth century, when Fazlallah was traveling around in search of converts. His personal claims following the enlightenment probably did invite the condemnation of some mainstream scholars, though this by itself cannot have led to suppression by the government. The true cause of the arrest and eventual execution was the political potential of Fazlallah's ideology and the growth of his following. The formation of a sizeable group around his charismatic personality was seen as a possible source of rebellion by the new government.

TIMUR-I LANG

Born into a lineage of chiefs of the Turkish Barlas tribe some time in the 1320s or 1330s, Timur distinguished himself as a charismatic and capable military man in his twenties. His father was a part of the ruling elite of the Chaghatay khanate in Central Asia. This political entity ruled over a mixed sedentary and nomadic population and had evolved out of the great Mongol empire that had, at one point in the thirteenth century, united China, Central Asia, the Middle East, and Eastern Europe under a single ruling house. Between the 1350s and 1380, Timur went from being a minor overlord of the region around the city of Kish (also known as Shahr-i Sabz) to becoming the biggest power in Central Asia. He received a severe leg wound during a battle in the early days of his ascendancy, which led to a limp and the enduring epithet Timur the Lame (Timur-i Lang), transformed into Tamerlane in European languages.

Although Timur spent his whole career as a systematic and ruthless conqueror, he never proclaimed himself a sovereign.

He maintained a puppet ruler from the lineage of the Mongol conqueror Chingiz Khan (d. 1227) at his capital and portrayed himself as the greatest among Turkish tribal chiefs. In 1368, he married the Mongol princess Saray Malik Khanim and came to be known as the son-in-law (*güregen*). Although this gave him some derivative legitimacy, Mongol traditions did not consider relatives by marriage a part of the dynasty and Timur respected this restriction throughout his life.

Despite his great ambition, Timur was a practical military man who worked according to precise plans when conquering regions, subjugating populations, and ensuring steady extraction of wealth from his vassals and subjects. He first became involved in the politics of Iran through alliances with dynasties that ruled the border regions with Central Asia. This eventually led to a ten-year period of planning a massive invasion of the Middle East that emulated the invasion of Chingiz Khan's grandson Hülegü in the middle of the thirteenth century. Over the period 1380 to 1400, he gradually brought most of the Middle East under his control through either direct attack and subjugation or by granting vassal status to local rulers in exchange for heavy ransoms and contributions to his forces.

The expansion of Timur's empire can be situated relative to Fazlallah Astarabadi's life by noting the years in which the major cities of Iran fell to his forces. The Sarbadar rulers of Sabzavar, with whom Fazlallah had contacts around 1360, allied themselves with Timur in 1381 and their domains were spared large-scale devastations. Despite a general immunity, some Sarbadar areas did see destruction, such as the city of Isfizar that was ransacked after a local rebellion in 1383. In 1384 during his first direct foray into central Iranian lands Timur conquered Astarabad, the city where Fazlallah was born in c. 1340. Tabriz, the scene of Fazlallah's enlightenment in 1374, fell to Timur's forces in 1386 and was made the capital of the whole of western Iran. Isfahan, a focus for Fazlallah's activity through the early 1370s, surrendered in 1388 and the city's population received particularly harsh treatment after some of Timur's tax collectors were killed upon entering the city. A historian recounts seeing at least twenty-eight towers of 1500 severed heads each outside the city's gates as an indication of the reprisal. In Timur's tactics, the overthrowing of the cities were often preceded by debilitating sieges and followed by devastating famines brought on by the conquerors' policies. It is understandable that populations faced with this sociopolitical situation would have been attracted to a charismatic religious leader like Fazlallah who claimed that the end of time was near and that the elect group who would accept him as the messiah would be delivered from the terrible situation in front of them in the near future.

Although he was nominally Muslim, Timur was not known for religious piety and we are not even sure where to place him in the framework of Islamic social entities such as sectarian groups, juridical schools, or Sufi orders. However, he almost always exempted religious professionals such as jurists, scholars, and dervishes from looting and torture at the hands of his forces when he captured a city. This attitude stemmed in part from prudence since such individuals were necessary for reestablishing the social order after the conquest. But Timur seems to have believed in the charismatic powers of particular religious men, some of whom he kept with him to provide advice or oracles. It was rare for Timur to intentionally cause the death of a charismatic religious man. If the person was seen as threatening rather than beneficial, he was simply banished from the realm without harm so that he could not gather a large following that would cause trouble. In this context, the arrest and execution of Fazlallah, a descendant of

Muhammad and a renowned charismatic dream interpreter, stands out as an anomaly rather than part and parcel of Timur's policies.

ARREST

Historians of the Timurid period who briefly mention Fazlallah state that he was arrested and executed in 804/1401–2. Works by Fazlallah's followers, on the other hand, unanimously place the event in 796/1394. This discrepancy can be solved in favor of 1394 since Fazlallah's followers were intimately concerned with the consequences of the death and no ideological reason can be identified that would have required changing the year. Furthermore, there is circumstantial evidence for preferring 1394. All sources agree that Timur's son Miranshah (d. 1408) carried out the sentence during his term as the governor of Azerbaijan. Miranshah was appointed to this post in 1393, at a time when Timur was campaigning in western Iran, and he was deposed in 1399 on suspicions of having become unduly independent. Fazlallah's arrest in 1394 was thus a part of the establishment of firm Timurid control over the region at the beginning of the rule of a new governor.

The historians state that Fazlallah was arrested after scholars of Samarqand and Gilan issued legal opinions that condemned him for religious innovation. Given the content of Fazlallah's thought, it is easy to see that mainstream scholars familiar with Fazlallah's claims would have passed such a judgment. However, opinions of this type are usually given at the behest of a governing authority and carry no weight without an agency willing to carry them out. In the context of Timur's empire in particular, scholars had very little influence over the conduct of state policy. The likeliest scenario is that Timur's government had found Fazlallah problematic and had imprisoned him. Scholars were then asked for an opinion that could be used to justify eliminating him completely. The case as a whole constituted a situation where the opinions of the scholars coincided very well with the interests of the Timurid state.

The arrest occurred at a time when Fazlallah was in the city of Shamakhi in Shirvan, a region today in the former Soviet republic of Azerbaijan. He had gone there to visit an associate named Qazi Bayazid who had been ill. This man told Fazlallah that he had seen a dream in which a person was being sacrificed and was fearful that this implied his impending death from the illness. Fazlallah reportedly consoled Qazi Bayazid by saying that the dream did not pertain to the illness but was actually a premonition of his own imminent death. True to form, Fazlallah was then arrested by the orders of Shaykh Ibrahim, the local authority in Shamakhi, just as he stepped out of Qazi Bayazid's house and was imprisoned along with one or more associates.

Fazlallah may well have foreseen that he would die a martyr because of his sense of his place in history as indicated in his interpretation of dreams in Shamakhi and other places. However, the way Shaykh Ibrahim is portrayed in the works of Fazlallah's followers indicates that Fazlallah was taken by surprise at the actual moment of arrest in Shirvan. The captor is constantly referred to as a traitor who betrayed the trust put in him by undertaking the arrest. There is some confusion about the precise chain of command that led to the arrest. Some works blame only Shaykh Ibrahim and Timur's son Miranshah and state that these two worked either without Timur's own knowledge of the matter or explicitly against him since he held Fazlallah in high regard. Others include Timur in their condemnations, referring to him as the "accursed lame demon" who had caused countless calamities for the whole population along with ordering Fazlallah's death. The arrest was very likely a minor matter in the overall scheme of Timur's activities and was carried out at the behest of the local authority, Miranshah, in a general sweep aimed at eliminating subversive elements from Timur's new Iranian domains.

LAST WILL AND TESTAMENT

Two versions of Fazlallah's last will and testament are extant. The first is quite short and can be cited here in full:

> I have a heart filled with desire for speech but no messenger can be found to convey it to you. God is witness to the situation of this poor unfortunate man, and no anxiety remains save regarding the scattering of his children and separation from his friends. Some matters that were pending are left to that dear friend and other dear ones. If God almighty wishes well for all, things will happen, either now or some time in the future.
> O Lord, O Lord of my nights:
> All my life I never found a single friend in Shirvan
> What to say of a friend, even a (sincere) acquaintance
> remained a mere wish
> I am the Husayn of the age, and the unworthy
> enemies my Shimr and Yazid
> My life is altogether 'Ashura and Shirvan my Karbala
> It is not hidden from those dear friends that this wretch harbors no anxieties in matters concerning religion. They are to convey my greetings and prayers at this last moment to my companions and friends and are to act such that these rules, verses, and truths, reach them. They are to settle down in some unknown corner for a while. This is the new command. Let them inquire from me about that child and others who remain and are free. Farewell.

This document contains mythological as well as real-life features conveying Fazlallah's feelings in the period after the arrest. The fact that he compares himself to Husayn indicates that he saw the calamity to have befallen him as a part of the larger battle between good and evil. Husayn was Muhammad's grandson who, in 680, was killed along with a number of his followers in Karbala, southern Iraq, because of his opposition to the rule of Yazid, the caliph belonging to the early Islamic Umayyad dynasty. In the centuries following Husayn's death, Muslims, particularly those belonging to the Shi'i sect, came to see Husayn as the ultimate martyr who gave his own life for the redemption of his followers. Conversely, the caliph Yazid, and Shimr, the Umayyad commander who fought against Husayn, became the ultimate human faces of wrongdoing.

The remainder of the document is concerned with more mundane matters, namely, the settlement of his affairs and the injunction to his family and followers to go into hiding. The larger version of the testament provides more details regarding these aspects, although the only existing copy of this version is garbled and not fully comprehensible. Nonetheless, we can tell that the testament was addressed to Fazlallah's eldest son Salamallah, whom he also designated the executor of all his affairs and the guardian of the family. He was to accomplish his charge in consultation and collaboration with a number of Fazlallah's close associates. This testament also mentions two or three women who appear to be Fazlallah's wives, other sons besides Salamallah, and daughters named 'A'isha and Fatima. Fazlallah in fact had more children than these who are referred to in the testament in general as sons and daughters without specifying names.

In the longer testament, Fazlallah enjoins members of his family to follow the advice of Salamallah and Fazlallah's senior followers. He tells his children as well as his followers to make themselves inconspicuous by avoiding any public display of their religious practice or their affiliation with Fazlallah. They are told to remove themselves to remote places so that people sent out to capture Fazlallah's associates would not be able to trace them. The children in particular were to disperse to different locations in the company of designated trustworthy followers so that even if one were caught, the authorities would not be able to eliminate the whole family en masse. Two of the daughters were also to be married to specific followers if the latter were still living.

The commands given in the larger testament are remarkable for their details. Although downcast because of the arrest, Fazlallah appears here as a realist concerned primarily with assuring the safety of his family and friends in a straightforward and practical way. The document refers to financial matters as well, though the details of these cannot be deciphered fully. Irrespective of his sense that his life was a part of cosmic mythology, it appears that, at least at this point in his life, Fazlallah was a man of the world fully concerned with managing his earthly affairs. His worldly attitude in evidence here is also a far cry from the austere life seen in stories from the time before his enlightenment.

EXECUTION

Fazlallah was shifted to the fortress of Alinjaq in the Nakhchivan region close to Shirvan soon after the arrest and was executed on the sixth day of the month of Zu l-Qaʻda, 796 (September 2, 1394). Some sources state that Miranshah carried out the beheading personally due to the severity of Fazlallah's crimes. Given the scant attention afforded him in official histories, he was probably not a huge threat and the idea that Miranshah acted as the executioner seems to be a legend. However, the governor's implication in the order that led to the death made him the ultimate villain in the eyes of Fazlallah's followers. Their works usually refer to him as Maranshah, or king of snakes, rather than by his actual name.

Fazlallah's followers had been shocked by the news of his arrest and an elegy by 'Ali al-A'la paints the picture of a community stricken with unbearable grief when it heard of the execution. The process of trying to make sense of the death began immediately since 'Ali al-A'la notes that observers had commented on the inauspicious astrological omens that were proliferating immediately before the event. The body was handed over to his followers and they were able to conduct a proper funeral and burial. The elegy says that for the followers, the sight of the coffin leaving their midst to be taken to the grave felt like the separation of their souls from their bodies. As discussed in a later chapter, Fazlallah's grave eventually became the movement's major shrine. It was seen as a piece of heaven on earth since devotees visiting it heard the dirt surrounding it echoing with the sounds of the winds of paradise.

Fazlallah's arrest and death were accompanied by a rounding up of at least some of his followers as well. His disciple Sayyid Kamal al-Din Husayn is identified specifically as a martyr who perished along with Fazlallah in the debacle. Some of his children did follow the advice of Fazlallah's testament and escaped to other regions such as Syria. The death may have shocked and saddened Fazlallah's followers but it did not lessen their faith in his status and teachings. However, they were forced to reinterpret the significance of his life in light of the new situation. Their efforts in this regard eventually led to a number of different options espoused by the various factions in the community. Fazlallah's religious system as represented in his written works and propagated by his disciples ensured that his legacy would live on long past his death. We now turn to Fazlallah's religious ideas before picking up the historical thread of the development of his movement after his death in Chapter 6.

4

COSMOS AND HUMANITY

Fazlallah Astarabadi's religious worldview put particular emphasis on the genealogy and history of the cosmos and the human species. Following previous Islamic as well as pre-Islamic religious systems, Fazlallah saw the cosmos and the human being as parallel entities, one being the macrocosm and the other the microcosm. The two systems were fundamentally interdependent so that to understand the microcosm one had to investigate the macrocosm, and vice versa. Fazlallah maintained that the interconnection between the two was grounded in the fact that both were aspects of God's self-manifestation in the material world.

The macrocosm was a display of God's attributes, traces, and acts, and constituted an array of signs that pointed to God. The human being, the microcosm, was the only created being capable of fully comprehending these signs. Human beings' highest calling in their earthly lives was to recognize the potential implanted in them in this regard and work toward its actualization. Taking their cues from heavenly scriptures and the spiritual experiences of prophets and saints among them, they were expected to decipher the cosmic mystery by understanding the unifying symbolic structure underlying its apparent multiplicity and disorganization. The ultimate purpose of human existence was thus to decode observable reality, through which humans came to understand God, the world, and themselves. Human beings who understood the cosmos and human existence possessed a portion of God's knowledge and, like God himself, came to see the manifest world as an aspect of their own beings. According to Fazlallah and his followers, he was the only human being to have achieved this in its totality so that he bridged the gap between humanity and divinity. He could, therefore, be addressed with titles such as "lord of all the worlds" that were usually reserved for God alone.

In Fazlallah's view, the intertwined destinies of the cosmos and the human species were one part predetermined and another part open to change based on deliberate action. The predetermined side of things resulted from the fact that God had created the world at a particular moment and with a determined purpose that would be fulfilled after it had exhausted its term. The lifespan of the world – the time between its creation and the final apocalypse – was also expected to unfold in cycles of time with known outlines. On the other hand, the willful, and hence changeable, dimension of the world depended on the way human beings responded to messages revealed to them through special messengers. To act appropriately, humans needed to know not only the static structure of time but also what particular time period they themselves were living in. The second imperative required intensive use of their intellectual and spiritual faculties for deciphering the signs of the times and recognizing the spiritual elect who were alive at that time and who deserved their allegiance. Fazlallah believed that what he had experienced in his life pointed to the fact that he himself was the final divinely appointed messenger for humanity. The whole metaphysical and historical system thus converged on his person since all people alive in his times were supposed to recognize him as the bearer of truth just before a final apocalyptic destruction of the cosmos.

These basic orientations regarding time, material reality, and God recur consistently throughout Fazlallah's works and the derivative interpretations found in the works of his followers. However, the details of the stories used to substantiate this mode of understanding existence vary considerably in the sources. The intellectual viewpoint of Fazlallah and his disciples is consistent with respect to the *methodology* used to understand the world, but their works do not contain a single *mythology* across the board. For example, the works contain a number of divergent narratives explaining the creation of the world that, despite their differences, indicate a consistent overall intellectual agenda. As a result of this factor, it is possible to encapsulate the general perspective with the help of a few examples.

The overall framework of Fazlallah Astarabadi's religious worldview can be summarized by concentrating on three themes: (1) the details of his views regarding the creation and evolution of the world as a whole (the macrocosm); (2) the particular position of the human species, the microcosm, within the created world; and (3) the structure of cosmic time, defined by various cycles, that was reaching its final conclusion during Fazlallah's lifetime. Fazlallah's religious vision is considerably richer than these three elements, but virtually everything he elaborates on rests on the foundation of these three concerns. The ideas discussed below had descriptive as well as prescriptive import for Fazlallah and his followers. The worldview described here enabled them to make sense of the world and, in conjunction with their historical circumstances and their personal religious inspirations, it provided them the basis for making decisions about how to act.

THE MACROCOSM

Fazlallah's discussion of the cosmos as a whole contains a particular emphasis on cosmogony, or the story of the creation of the world. As mentioned several times already, he felt that he was living at the end of time and, as in other religious ideologies centered on apocalyptic ideas, to understand the dissolution of the world one had to know about its creation. His interpretation of the creation was a particular version of the genesis story as it is found in the Qur'an and its Jewish and Christian antecedents. Following a view popular among Sufis, he stated that the ultimate reason for the existence of the cosmos was God's desire to be known. Before the beginning of time, God, the uncreated being who has always existed, felt lonely and decided to create entities other than himself so that he would become an object of knowledge. He then set the process of creation into motion through the command "be," which produced the fundaments of the cosmos out of nothing (Q. 2: 117, 3: 47, 6: 73, 19: 35, 40: 68).

In Fazlallah's view, the scriptural report that God *said* "be" was to be taken quite literally. God was to be seen as actually articulating a word in a form of language to produce the world. Because of this primordial event, language and materiality were fundamentally interconnected throughout all later phases of the world's continuing existence. The actual sound of God's word and the material produced from the command were facets of the same event, and the moment of creation was in fact a bifurcation of divine attributes leading to a constant relationship between sounds and bodies in the cosmos. The cosmos as a whole – seen as a conglomeration of materials and sounds – was thus an echo of the word "be," with all entities and movements representing continuing reverberations of the divine command issued at the beginning of time.

God's creative activity continued after the first command and he gradually brought all aspects of the material cosmos into existence. The creation of the cosmos reached its apex and conclusion when God kneaded clay from a mixture of the elements earth and water with his hands and imprinted the lump in front of him with an image of himself. In Qur'anic terminology, this event was represented in the idea that, after he had created the heavens and the earth in six days, God "seated himself upon the throne" (10: 3, 13: 2, 20: 5, 25: 59, 32: 4, 57: 4). The clay model that resulted from the act of imprinting was the human body, that of Adam, which God then proceeded to enhance by giving it life and knowledge. He animated it by blowing into it some of his own spirit (Q. 32: 10) and endowed it with a share of his knowledge before presenting it to angels as an object of veneration (Q. 2: 31–4, 7: 11, 17: 61, 18: 50, 20: 116). God commanded the angels to bow down in front of Adam by telling them that he was more exalted than them because he knew the "names of things" that had not been divulged to the angels. Once fully assembled, Adam was the being most similar to God in all of creation since his bodily form was an imprint of God, he was infused with God's spirit, and God had made him privy to knowledge withheld from other beings.

At this juncture in the narrative of creation, Adam became subject to the hostility of Iblis or Satan, the angel or jinn who refused to bow before him because of a feeling of superiority. For Fazlallah and his followers, it was particularly noteworthy that Iblis's objection to Adam was based on his contention that the element fire, which formed his own body, was superior to the clay that constituted Adam's body (Q. 7: 12). The material content of the bodies of a species was therefore always a noteworthy matter for understanding its place from the very beginning of the drama of the cosmos. Iblis's mistake was that he had considered fire superior to earth and water and God's reprisal against him pointed out that the truth was the exact opposite of his contention.

For Fazlallah, the "names" taught to Adam that compelled all angels except Iblis to bow down in front of him were the letters of an alphabet that allowed him to comprehend the world. The letters in question were, however, not the entities familiar to us from knowing any of the readily available writing systems. They were the fundamental constituents of the very language that God had used when he had said "be" to create the world. What had been imparted to Adam was not a particular language but the more general capacity for language, represented by a kind of metalanguage, which was necessary for first creating the world and then comprehending it. God had no use for language before creating the cosmos since he was alone and did not need to communicate with any other being. The utterance "be" was the first instance of language, from which all other aspects of language such as sounds and letters came into being. Fazlallah claimed that the "names" taught to Adam were the thirty-two sound-letter pairs that formed the alphabet of this divine metalanguage. Through these God had imparted the greatest cosmic secrets to the human species.

By endowing Adam with the metalinguistic alphabet, God had made him capable of understanding the cosmos. The combination of sound and material was said to inhere in everything in the created sphere so that all entities in the mineral, vegetable, and animal kingdoms had sounds peculiar to them. Among these, the human being was unique since its vocal cords were not restricted to a single characteristic sound but could articulate the sounds of all entities. Here too, it was crucial that Adam's abilities were not merely spiritual but had a direct connection to the constitution of his body. The high station accorded to Adam in this interpretation of the creation of the world formed the basis for much of the rest of Fazlallah's religious pronouncements.

THE MICROCOSM

Following the initial period of cosmic generation, Adam and his spouse Eve were made the progenitors of a whole species. Fazlallah's works do not dwell on the human fall from grace through the instigation of Iblis. Instead, he presumes that God had created humans as beings who had the potential to recognize and know him. Their placement on earth as a trial was thus not an accident but part of the plan from the very beginning.

Fazlallah saw the story of Adam's creation as the production of the prototype for the human species as a whole. The imprinted clay that formed Adam's body acted as the mold for the creation of later humans, and the production of each member of the species replicated God's intentions toward the species. Since the human being was the microcosm, the conception, maturation, and eventual demise of every individual human reiterated the story of the cosmos from genesis to final dissolution. The story began in the womb of the mother where the embryo was generated through the intermixing of male and female fluids. The moment of fertilization was equivalent to God's command "be" in the macrocosmic perspective. During the period of gestation, the embryo successively acquired parts such as blood, nerves, arteries, and bones, leading up to the fully constituted human body. The process of the formation of these parts was equal to the first six days of initial creation when God had constructed the heavens and the earth. Once the body was complete, a spirit was blown into it, reenacting God's action with respect to Adam on the seventh day of creation. Once fully developed, the normal brain function of the human being equaled the capacity for language that derived from the knowledge imparted to Adam in the form of the names and would prove crucial in later stages of development. The embryo then turned into a human infant when born into the world.

For Fazlallah, the body of every human infant bore the signs of God's speech in the form of seven lines of hair that marked its face. These were: the hairline, two eyebrows, and the two sets of eyelashes (four lines). These lines paralleled the seven verses of the first chapter of the Qur'an, The Opening. The idea here was again that God's creative commands existed in bifurcated forms in bodies and sounds in the physical world and that we could see the correspondences between the two facets by correlating major aspects of a body (the human being) with a form of speech (the Qur'an). The fact that these two entities in particular were comparable was no surprise since they were, respectively, the best body and the most perfect form of materialized language, God's ultimate scripture.

The maturation of the human body in the years after the birth also contained clues to the connection between body and speech/text. This could be seen in the arrival of more lines of hair on the human face, though the way this occurred was different for males and females. On the male face, the appearance of facial hair increased the number to fourteen: two lines each on cheeks, above the moustache, and below the lips, and one at the end of the beard. The female face itself did not acquire seven additional lines, but it had an equivalent in the female's capacity to give birth. Through this, another human face and its lines appeared in the world. Like the seven lines, the fourteen lines also paralleled an aspect of the text of the Qur'an. Some chapters of the Qur'an begin with groups of letters that do not constitute actual words. These random letters have been a source of much speculation by Muslims over the centuries, with little consensus regarding their true meaning or significance. Fazlallah observed that, eliminating repetition, this group as a whole consists of fourteen separate letters. This feature of the Qur'an is not obvious and has to be deduced, just as the human being does not have the additional seven lines at birth and develops them in the process of maturation.

In the case of both males and females, Fazlallah saw the fourteen lines as seals that sat on top of the places on the face where they occurred. Consequently, the significant entities that "inhabited" the face were in fact twenty-eight: fourteen lines and the fourteen places on the face on which the lines sat as seals. In parallel, the text of the Qur'an was revealed in Arabic, whose alphabet contained twenty-eight letters. In a given human life cycle, the number twenty-eight was reached as a result of the process of becoming an adult. Similarly, the Qur'an, with its twenty-eight letters, was the last scripture and had appeared in the world at a late stage in cosmic history.

The human being's status as a reflection of God's speech was affirmed when the male acquired facial hair and the female gave birth during teenage years. Up to this point, the person him- or herself could not interfere with the lines and the processes involved were natural. Women's bearing children was socially normative and would have been perceived as a natural course of things in their life cycles. Going beyond these steps, Fazlallah contended that it was a universal human trait to part the hair of the head and, in the case of the male, of the beard into two sides. This revealed one or two more lines and the places underneath them. Parting the hair was an act of volition, here representing a deliberate attempt to adorn oneself, thereby becoming better and civilized. It was in fact seen as the point of becoming fully human since it was only now that the face became a dwelling place of thirty-two entities – sixteen lines and sixteen places under them – in parallel with the thirty-two letters that God had taught Adam as the names at the beginning of creation. With this, each human face came to reflect God's speech in its entirety following maturation as well as deliberate cultivation. This fundamental fact underlying the correlation between divine speech and the human body was affirmed also by the fact that the mature human mouth, the organ that actually produced speech, contained a total of thirty-two teeth.

The single line that parted the hair to create the fully human person was seen as a mark of God's creativity that was evident throughout nature. It could be observed in the following single lines: the slit that reveals the eye, the nose that divides the face, the line between the lips that reveals the mouth cavity, the line in the middle of every seed of grain, the line that naturally divides the mane of the horse, the line that splits the lower lip of the camel, etc. In all these cases, the single line was seen as God's imprint on the bodies in question, recalling, among other things, the singleness of God's essence and the production of the pair of materiality and sound through God's command "be" in the first moment of genesis. The fundamental unity of the cosmos and the parity between the macrocosm and the microcosm were reflected also in the fact that the eight final lines on all human faces (hairline, two eyebrows, four eyelashes, parting in head hair) multiplied by the four elements (earth, wind, water, fire) reflected the thirty-two names/letters God had taught Adam in the beginning.

Human beings were bearers of language both in the forms of their bodies and in their intellectual ability to acquire spoken and written speech. The general capability was turned into a specific form by learning particular human languages and alphabets. These languages gave humans the ability to comprehend the world and communicate with each other through symbolic means, something not available to other created beings. However, these languages were limited in scope compared to the metalanguage taught to Adam at the moment of creation.

The metalanguage, with its thirty-two letters, did not represent or symbolize reality but named it from its very essence.

Fazlallah's view of this language was articulated in the oft-repeated statement "the [metalinguistic] name of a thing is its very essence". This maxim followed from the fact that, on one side of the equation, the names of all physical, imaginary, and conceptual entities rested ultimately on the primordial metalanguage. All things named were, therefore, predicated fundamentally on its set of thirty-two letters as a whole. On the other side, the essence of a thing was that element whose absence necessitated a complete lack of the thing itself. The essence was the metalinguistic name of the entity since it was the only element unequivocally necessary for the entity to exist at all. If this were not so, the thing would fall outside the purview of the metalanguage, which was impossible. Once again, the crucial inference to be drawn from this argument was that the universe was fundamentally a linguistic event. As the creator, God had complete mastery over the metalanguage while he had endowed human beings with the possibility of acquiring it. The base potential for this to happen was discernible in humans' everyday ability to comprehend and vocalize ordinary languages and decipher various alphabets. However, the true appreciation of the cosmic mystery required transcending these languages and becoming aware of the metalanguage and "recalling" its thirty-two letters/names revealed to Adam in primordial time and lying dormant within every human being. Fazlallah believed that the spiritual matters revealed to him formed a pathway toward recalling this metalanguage. He was the only person with the full ability to translate between ordinary languages and the metalanguage, and the task of his audience was to master his works and to emulate him in order to decipher their own existence and the surrounding world.

COSMIC TIME

The description of Fazlallah's ideas so far has highlighted the salience of the physical human body and its deep connections to God's intentions in creating the world. Along with rationalizing the individual human life cycle, Fazlallah also believed that the cosmos was destined to go through three cycles of time between its creation and final destruction. This represented the lifespan of the macrocosm and paralleled the development of the human microcosm from birth to death. The beginnings, ends, and intervening points of the three cycles were tied to the appearance into the world of particularly significant prophets and saints. The cosmic term as a whole was geared toward a gradual unfolding of God's plan for the created world.

Fazlallah divided cosmic time into a tripartite scheme consisting of cycles of prophecy, sainthood, and divinity. The prophetic cycle began with Adam and ended with Muhammad; the cycle of sainthood began with 'Ali and ended with Fazlallah; and the divine cycle began with Fazlallah's proclamations following his enlightenment and was expected to end with an imminent final apocalypse. Events within each cycle could be placed relative to the markers of the boundaries between them and the stories of prophets told in the scriptures all pointed to this scheme. Fazlallah's works contain extensive discussions of all Qur'anic narratives about prophetic figures and his general attitude to them can be illustrated by concentrating on his views on Adam, Eve, Mary, Jesus, and Muhammad.

Adam's significance has already been discussed in the section on cosmogony and it suffices here that he figures prominently as the founder of the cycle of prophecy and the father of the species. Eve's significance lay in the fact that she was the actual bearer of the species, the primordial mother. She was, in one sense, inferior to Adam since he was created first and acted as the mold for her creation. However, she was equal to Adam and necessary for his fulfillment in that the cosmos could not progress along its predestined course without her. After the generation of the first two human beings with their differentiated reproductive capabilities, the coupling of human males and females represented a constant transfer of lines from one side to the other. The seven lines on all human faces were called the "motherly" lines, and those that appeared later on male faces were known as the "fatherly" lines. The two sets were interdependent on each other in a kind of cycle: the male began with the seven motherly lines and developed to fourteen at puberty when the seven fatherly lines appeared on his face; the fatherly lines were then transferred to a woman through sexual intercourse; and she then gave birth to a child who had the motherly lines on his or her face. The cycle established by the coupling of Adam and Eve thus continued from generation to generation.

All humans descended from Adam and Eve replicated the numerical patterns leading to thirty-two discussed above until Jesus, who was anomalous because he was born without a father and through a divine command "be" addressed directly to Mary's womb. His thirty-two lines were not derived from two parents, but this was amply compensated for by the fact that he was, literally, the word of God become flesh. This was significant because in the previous cases, all humans reflected the thirty-two letters of the metalanguage in the parallel but disconnected systems of the body and the language. However, as a direct materialization of God's word, Jesus' body *was* the exteriorization of the all-pervasive metalanguage, a situation that differed from all other human beings.

In addition, Jesus' birth commenced an internal cycle of time within the prophetic cycle that contained a special exteriorization of the divine metalanguage in the human sphere.

Jesus' teachings were the first step in this direction, although Fazlallah's perspective underscored that these were not fully understood in his own time. Their full significance could be seen only through the further unfolding of the cycle of prophecy. The text of the New Testament was thus laden with meanings that had been overlooked by Christians. Muhammad and his Muslim followers understood this scripture better since they had arrived later in history, and Fazlallah could now provide the final and deepest understanding.

After Jesus, the next important human person to arrive in the world was, of course, the Prophet Muhammad, whose body was nothing out of the ordinary. What he brought, however, was the Qur'an, God's speech in the form of the twenty-eight letters of the Arabic script. What Jesus' body represented in its flesh was found in the letters and sounds of the Qur'an. The textual form was superior to the corporeal since it was more easily comprehensible by the human mind. Although the Qur'an was easier to "read" than the body of Jesus, it was still a highly allusive text that required interpretation. The Qur'an was said to have seven levels of meanings in each part of the text, of which only the simplest and least significant was accessible in the literal meanings attached to the Arabic words that could be understood by someone who knew the language.

In Fazlallah's understanding, deeper investigation and interpretation of the Qur'an were the chief religious activities of the cycle of sainthood, which began with 'Ali and ended with Fazlallah's enlightenment. Twelver Shi'i Imams and great Sufi masters from the dawn of Islam to the time of Fazlallah's own proclamations were the chief luminaries of this cosmic cycle.

Fazlallah marked the transition from the cycle of sainthood to the third and final cycle of divinity. He was the consummation of all processes of cosmic history. He was given the gift of the complete understanding of all the scriptures, particularly the Qur'an, and felt that, following his enlightenment experience, his body had become the repository of the thirty-two letters of the metalanguage. These had descended into him in a revelation and had made his bodily presence comparable to that of Jesus who was a direct representation of God's speech. It is possible that Fazlallah saw this parallel between himself and Jesus as the metaphorical realization of the idea of Jesus' Second Coming accepted by most Muslims.

One of Fazlallah's ultimate proofs for asserting his status as the culmination of history was the fact that he proclaimed himself in Persian, a language that had an alphabet with thirty-two letters. Because of this numerical parallel with the primordial alphabet, Persian was seen as the closest correlate to the original metalanguage taught to Adam. Fazlallah's works are most thoroughly imbued with Qur'anic quotations, and taken together, they can be considered an extended Persian commentary on the Arabic scripture. Comparing Fazlallah to the evolution of the macrocosmic sphere, one sees that his writings were like the parting of the hair of the head and the beard that takes the human face from its natural state to becoming a full reflection of the thirty-two letters of the metalanguage. What shone forth from his writings was the ultimate truth of the cosmos, revealed at a time when the macrocosm had reached its maturation. He himself as the writer, and those among his followers who had absorbed his works, were the consummate human beings, images of God's command "be" in both body and knowledge. At the moment of the creation of the cosmos, the creative utterance had bifurcated into materiality and sound. With Fazlallah's understandings, the perfection of the body was rejoined with the metalanguage, thus realizing God's ultimate purpose in creating the cosmos. By acquiring and embodying the metalanguage, Fazlallah and his followers satisfied God's desire for beings who would know him.

Fazlallah's supporters were exceptional human beings since the maturation of their bodies and minds coincided with the maturation of the cosmos as a whole. Because of the times in which they lived, the microcosm and the macrocosm were becoming combined in their beings. This was, on the one hand, a matter of fate since God had fixed the course of cosmic history from the very beginning. On the other hand, an understanding of their status necessitated that they act in the world in keeping with their cosmic role. This imperative compelled them to reflect on religious matters, write explanatory narratives, and travel widely to proclaim themselves. Fazlallah's idea that he was the messenger of universal salvation before an imminent apocalypse left him no choice but to seek the maximum number of believers in the shortest possible time. The fact that a substantial number of his contemporaries were willing to accept his claims eventually led to his death at the hands of his Timurid captors in 1394.

5

APOCALYPSE, LANGUAGE, AND SALVATION

By the time of Fazlallah Astarabadi's activity, apocalyptic religious ideas had had a long history as a part of the Islamic tradition. Derived originally from Jewish, Christian, and Zoroastrian antecedents, these ideas projected that time was linear and that its end would see the final great struggle between good and evil. It was expected that a messiah would lead the forces of truth, and that he would be opposed by antichrist-like figures known under names such as Dajjal or Dabba (the beast). Muslims in the first two centuries of the Islamic era (c. 600–800) were divided into hostile groups that both fought against each other in battlefields and tried to justify their positions through intellectual effort. In the course of the latter endeavor, they assimilated the messianic ideas already current in the region, thereby turning them into a distinctive Islamic system.

The rich and highly imaginative eschatological ideas in the traditions of the first two centuries formed the basis for the dogmas of the Islamic sects that solidified in the classical period (c. 800–1200), in so far as they were not rejected. Messianic and apocalyptic doctrines varied considerably between different sects and subsects, and they were also regarded with skepticism by a number of people throughout Islamic history. The contested nature of messianic ideas meant that anyone who wished to discuss the topic could count on criticism from many directions.

Muslims like Fazlallah, who lived after the classical period, had both the corpus of early apocalyptic traditions and the standardized messianic dogmas of the different sects at their disposal. Out of these ideas, Fazlallah devised new configurations so that his interpretation of the apocalypse as a whole was unique in its specific details. His beliefs are most closely related to those of Shi'i Muslims belonging to the Twelver (also known as Imami), the Isma'ili, and the Ghulat ("exaggerator") subsects. These Shi'is had a heavy investment in apocalyptic and messianic ideas because they considered early Islamic history a tragedy and expected that the world would finally be set right when the messiah made his appearance at the end of time. By the fourteenth century, when Fazlallah proclaimed himself as the messiah, the Twelver and Ghulat subsects had turned their messiahs into mythological figures whose appearance in the flesh was not usually considered imminent. Some types of Isma'ili Shi'is (Musta'lis) believed in a similarly abstracted messiah while others (Nizaris) followed a living Imam who was not regarded as the Mahdi and who was politically quiescent.

Fazlallah attempted to blow new life into the messianic paradigm by showing how the stories and scenarios contained in existing traditions applied to the circumstances of his own life. During the fourteenth and fifteenth centuries, the eastern Islamic world saw the rise of a number of other messianic movements as well. Fazlallah's innovative interpretation of the various existing messianic paradigms paralleled the thought of other messiahs such as Muhammad Nurbakhsh (d. 1464), Muhammad b. Falah Musha'sha' (d. 1462), and leaders of the Safavid Sufi order active in the last three decades of the fifteenth century. A generally heightened concern with messianism could be seen also in the history of the Sarbadar state (discussed in Chapter 2) and in numerous other historical incidents reported in the period's chronicles. Fazlallah's messianic claim was thus part of a larger pattern in the religious history of the Islamic east during the late medieval period.

Fazlallah's specific view of the apocalypse divided the event into two phases. The first phase corresponded with the literal meaning of apocalypse (a cosmic unveiling or revelation), which he thought referred to his own enlightenment, while the second phase signified the cataclysmic destruction popularly associated with the end of time. The physical dissolution of the universe indicated by the second phase of the apocalypse was expected to occur after Fazlallah had fulfilled his earthly role as the messiah.

Fazlallah's works were concerned primarily with the first phase of the apocalypse since he was keen to prove that he had become privy to special revealed knowledge. The apocalypse was, in this sense, a mental change of perspective, and to participate in it meant seeing everything from a new angle. The physical world had not changed as yet but people exposed to Fazlallah's interpretation were expected to see it with new eyes. Thereafter they were expected to experience the physical destruction at the end of time as a confirmation of the destruction of ordinary perception that had taken place in their minds. Adopting the mental apocalypse offered by Fazlallah was crucial for one's salvation since that way one became a conscious participant in the historical process instead of being its unwitting victim.

Appreciating Fazlallah's understanding of the apocalypse requires familiarizing oneself with the system of interpretation found in his own works and the derivative literature produced by his followers. Ideas about the cosmos, the human species, and time discussed in Chapter 4 constitute the bases for this system. The actual implementation of the system is visible most clearly in the way Fazlallah and his followers understood the components and functions of language. In the following discussion, I treat their overall view of language and their explanations for why it was necessary to investigate linguistic phenomena such as sounds, letters, words, and narratives in many different ways to understand the nature of the apocalypse. The end of the chapter explains how Fazlallah's interpretation of language connected concretely to human salvation.

RELIGIOUS LINGUISTICS

In Fazlallah's perception, all tangible reality was a materialization of the divine metalanguage. The sounds of the cosmos were the spoken aspect of this metalanguage and the physical world its written aspect. The metalanguage had been revealed to Fazlallah and he could understand all of existence by hearing and reading the cosmos. His teachings for other human beings amounted to instruction in the metalanguage; the more it became a part of one's consciousness, the better one understood the cosmos and one's own place within it.

The metalanguage could not be taught like ordinary human languages since the latter are symbolic systems that work by assigning signifying sounds to material or conceptual entities. For example, someone who understands English knows that the utterance produced by combining the sounds d-o-g signifies a particular animal. There is no inherent connection between the signifying sounds and the signified animal, and the association between the two has to be learned by someone who wishes to understand English. In the metalanguage, the signifier and the signified had an inherent relationship since Fazlallah claimed that the metalinguistic name of a thing was its very essence.

One significant proof for this assertion was the fact that the ordinary letters of the alphabet are the only material entities whose names have to contain a reference to the named entities. For example, writing the name of the first letter of the alphabet, *alif*, requires using the letter *alif* itself. Similarly, the name *alif* cannot be pronounced without using the sound associated with the letter *alif*. The letters of the alphabet are the only existent entities for which the signifiers and the signified are inextricably connected. For entities other than letters, there is no essential connection between names in ordinary languages and the things named (e.g. "dog" in spoken or written form has no necessary connection to a particular animal). Ordinary letters were thus the closest correlates to the metalinguistic letters that were the essence of all existence.

One interesting aspect of this scheme was that individual letters/sounds of ordinary languages provided the strongest connection to the metalanguage although they did not carry linguistic meaning in ordinary languages themselves. Conversely, once these letters and sounds were combined to form words, they acquired ordinary linguistic meaning but lost their close association with the metalinguistic letters. This revealed a fundamental disjuncture between the metalanguage and ordinary languages, indicating that one could not "translate" from one side to the other as could be done between two ordinary languages. The only way to get to the metalanguage from ordinary languages was to break words down to letters and sounds and analyze them to see their metalinguistic referents. This was precisely the job of Fazlallah's "science of letters" (*'ilm-i huruf*), abundantly in evidence in all the literature stemming from his movement. The science relied on a number of different techniques for breaking and reconstituting language that were learned through careful study of Fazlallah's works. The cumulative knowledge gained from understanding all the interpretations offered by Fazlallah was thought to train one into becoming a consummate listener and reader of the metalanguage.

The fundamental difference between the metalanguage and ordinary languages meant also that the two were apprehended through different human senses. While ordinary language was understood through ears and eyes, the requisite organ for the metalanguage was the heart, understood as the seat of intelligence. Metalinguistic letters related to the ordinary letters in the same way as a specimen of a species to its archetype (i.e. an actual dog to the concept dog that connotes the species as a whole). Based on this analogy, the metalinguistic letters were devoid of shapes and bodies and were to be thought of as abstract principles, while the ordinary letters of the various alphabets were derived from them through a concretizing process. An individual writer or speaker producing ordinary letters/sounds was thought to be involved in a partial apprehension of the metalinguistic letters. Instead of "generating" the letters, the use of a hand or a tongue to materialize language amounted to "uncovering" the metalinguistic letters present in the cosmos as its primary constituents. The production and apprehension of ordinary language occurred through physical senses while the metalanguage became understood through the inner human organ of the heart. Translating from one type of language to the other was, therefore, a journey to the core of the human being.

THE SCIENCE OF LETTERS

Fazlallah's science of letters was particularly concerned with two phenomena: human languages in their spoken and written forms, and the sounds and shapes of the cosmos that contained hidden references to sounds and letters. People outside Fazlallah's movement referred to him and his followers as Hurufis or "letterists" because of their obsession with investigating language in all its forms and seeing it reflected in all material reality.

Letter mysticism had long been a part of Islamic esoteric traditions such as Sufism and Shi'ism and a general concern with deciphering language at this level was not extraordinary in Fazlallah's times. Preserved discourses of the Shi'i Imams contain extensive discussions of letters, and the same is true of works by famous Sufi authors such as Ibn al-'Arabi (d. 1240) and Sa'd al-Din Humuvayi (d. 1252), among numerous others. There is in fact much similarity between Fazlallah's system and mainstream Sufism at the level of appreciating the centrality of language (particularly the text of the Qur'an) for discovering esoteric religious secrets. However, Sufis usually thought that the world contained an infinite number of divine signs and their explorations were, by necessity, only partial expositions of cosmic truths.

In addition to the esoteric traditions, the *abjad* system that gave a numerical value to each letter of the alphabet and then tried to extract meanings from words by performing mathematical calculations was common currency among all educated Muslims in the medieval period. Works by Fazlallah and his followers make use of this system only occasionally.

In historical terms, the speculation on letters, numbers, and geometric shapes was connected also to Pythagorean ideas of pre-Islamic provenance. Such notions had been particularly popular with philosophically inclined groups like the anonymous Brethren of Purity (Ikhwan al-Safa) who composed their encyclopedic *Epistles* (*Rasa'il*) sometime between the ninth and eleventh centuries. Such theorists thought that the cosmos was inherently symmetrical in mathematical and geometric terms and that this symmetry was observable in physical phenomena. Ideas proposed in the works of the Brethren of Purity and other like-minded groups found extensive use in Isma'ili Shi'i discussions between the tenth and thirteenth centuries.

Fazlallah's view of the letters and sounds of language differed from those of his predecessors in that he claimed to understand the whole system once and for all through the concept of the metalanguage. Earlier speculation had seen letters as signifiers pointing to God's knowledge, but Fazlallah connected them to the metalinguistic letters that were the basis for all material existence. The totalizing scope of Fazlallah's assertions regarding his letter interpretation reflected the idea that he was the messiah who had received the ultimate revelation before the end of time. He believed that although all that could be heard and seen in sentient experience stemmed from the metalanguage, the sounds and written words of ordinary human languages were the clearest correlates to the metalanguage. Therefore, the spoken word and the written text were the most efficient gateways to the metalanguage and needed the greatest attention.

Of all materials available in ordinary languages, the Bible and the Qur'an were the most valuable since they were God's word. Their obvious linguistic meanings represented the least valuable forms of God's knowledge, but one could get to higher meanings by discovering the hidden levels – usually as many as seven – that lay underneath the obvious text. In addition to the sounds and letters ordinarily regarded as language, sounds and letters were to be seen to be present in the rest of the material cosmos as well. It was possible, therefore, to see any sound as a garbled form of human language and discover shapes of letters in the shapes of material objects. A consummate interpreter such as Fazlallah could understand all ordinary languages in spoken and written forms and could decipher matters such as the language of birds. When he looked at the physical world, he saw it permeated with the shapes of letters that could be read. The cosmos was thus an open book to him because of his mastery of the metalanguage.

FROM ARABIC TO PERSIAN

Although all languages were related to the metalanguage, Fazlallah believed that Arabic and Persian were closest to the ultimate truth. This was reflected in the fact that their alphabet had, respectively, twenty-eight and thirty-two letters, which were related to the lines that appear on the human face. The status of these languages was ratified also through Muhammad's supposed statement that Arabic and Persian were the languages of paradise.

The interrelationship between Arabic and Persian was of particular interest to Fazlallah since it ran parallel to the transition between the cycles of prophecy and divinity. Muhammad had been the last prophet and had received his revelation in Arabic, and Fazlallah was the ultimate interpreter and expressed himself in Persian. To substantiate this transition, Fazlallah and his followers relied on a hadith in which Muhammad was asked, "How is a prophet what he is?" He replied, "Through a book that descends to him." The inquisitor then asked what was the descended book, and he said the twenty-nine letters of the alphabet, meaning the twenty-eight Arabic letters and *lam-alif*. *Lam* and *alif* are two separate letters of the alphabet that were, in this hadith, joined together as a single entity and added to the alphabet.

In Fazlallah's system, the *lam-alif* as a single "letter" in the Arabic alphabet was the crucial marker predicting the change of language between the Qur'an and Fazlallah's works. The name of this letter contained four distinct letters / sounds: l-m-a-f. These four were seen as stand-ins for the four letters p-ch-zh-g that had to be added to the Arabic script to write Persian. During the prophetic cycle, a new prophet surpassed his predecessors by becoming the recipient of a new scripture. For example, Muhammad with his Qur'an had superseded the biblical prophets who had received the Hebrew Bible and the New Testament. But Fazlallah was not a mere prophet; rather, he marked the beginning of a whole new dispensation, the cycle of divinity. Consequently, he did not receive a new scripture but rather the key to the full understanding of the existing scriptures through the transition from Arabic to Persian. The possibility of this transition had always been hidden within Arabic through the idea of the *lam-alif* as a separate letter. With Fazlallah's knowledge, it became clear that now Persian had to be used to make sense of all linguistic data.

The idea that Persian transcended Arabic had direct consequences for interpreting the Qur'anic text. Besides writing commentaries on the Arabic text in Persian, Fazlallah and his followers maintained that the Arabic text itself could actually be read as if it were Persian. This possibility was visible in an interpretation given in an epistle by one of Fazlallah's followers named Mir Fazili. This author (about whom we know nothing besides this work) was concerned with interpreting Qur'an 30: 2–4, which reads: "The Byzantines have been vanquished in the nearer part of the land; and, after their vanquishing, they shall be the victors in a few years" (*ghulibat ar-rum; fi adna l-ard wa-hum min ba'di ghalabihim sayaghlabun; fi bid'i sinin*). Fazili explained that the word "*rum*," which in Arabic means Byzantium, should actually be read as "writing on the face" because its true referent is the Persian phrase "my face (*ruy-i man*)." His authority for this unconventional way of treating language was the Qur'anic verse that states, "(there is) nothing fresh or withered, but it is in a clear book" (6: 59), implying that all human languages could be related to the Qur'an in some shape or form.

Moving further in the interpretation of the verses, Fazili stated that, in its normal Arabic meaning, when one adds the definite article "*al-*" to the word "*rum*," the compound word (*al-rum*, pronounced *ar-rum*) meant the Byzantines, "inhabitants of Byzantium." Transferring now to Persian, he claimed that the true referents of the compound word *al-rum* were the "inhabitants of the human face," namely the seven lines. The Qur'anic text that follows was, then, a reference to the creation of Eve after Adam, because the Byzantines' "defeat in the nearer part of the land" meant the creation of a being lesser than Adam at a time after Adam's creation (defeat = lesser, nearer = later). Although Eve may be lesser than Adam, her existence was necessary for the start of the human species, and this species was the most crucial part of the cosmic plan since humans fulfilled the purpose of the cosmos by recognizing God. Eve's "deficiency" with respect to Adam, therefore, was in fact a marker of creation's perfection, and this was the meaning of the Qur'anic verse when it stated that the Byzantines would be victorious even after being defeated.

The last part of the Qur'anic text under discussion ("in a few years" [*fi bid'i sinin*]) was said to refer to the additional seven facial lines peculiar to males. The "few" in this case meant "seven," and the reference to years corresponded to the fact that males were born with only seven "motherly" lines common to all humans, but acquired the additional "fatherly" lines after a few years. The "victory" of the Byzantines also had an application here since the masculine lines came on top of the universal feminine ones.

Fazili's interpretation of these Qur'anic verses accorded well with the general principles of Fazlallah's science of letters. Fazlallah maintained that the letters and sounds of language were greater bearers of truth than the words formed from combining them. Fazili separated the letters/sounds of the Qur'an from their Arabic meanings and read/heard them in Persian, the new sacred language. The overall operation was thus consistent with the science of letters propounded in Fazlallah's thought.

In addition to emphasizing Persian, Fazlallah may have believed that all linguistic phenomena in one language can be treated as if they were in a different language to get to higher meanings. This can be deduced from a vision recounted in his *Book of Dreams* in which he saw someone reading the Qur'an in Turkish. The person was doing this not by translating the Arabic words into their Turkish equivalents but by mouthing the sounds of the Arabic text and then trying to see what these sounds might mean if the text were in Turkish. The possibility of such "readings" of the Qur'an could be justified by the contention that the sounds of the Qur'an were not confined to Arabic but conveyed meaning in all human languages.

The innovative nature of Fazlallah's general approach to language should be evident from these examples. He used the purported connection between the metalanguage and ordinary languages to disassociate existing texts/speech from their conventional meanings. This method freed Fazlallah and his followers from the literal meanings of the scriptures. Moreover, it was precisely this aspect of his thought that was most threatening for scholars invested in conventional interpretations of religion. Mainstream Muslim scholars saw the text of the Qur'an as the most secure source of guidance for their intellectual and practical concerns. Through his radical ideas, Fazlallah wholly undermined the stability of the text and the entire religious system founded on it.

OPERATIONS ON LETTERS

Along with re-reading the Qur'an in various ways, Fazlallah and his followers also scrutinized the letters of the Perso-Arabic alphabet on an individual basis. They believed that each letter/sound was a substantive doorway to the metalanguage. One author explained this with reference to the Persian statements "there is a God" (*khuda hast*) and "there is no God" (*khuda nist*). According to God's law, pronouncing the first statement made one deserving of paradise, while the second one led to execution and a life in hell. The crucial distinction between the meanings of the statements was embodied in the difference between the letters "h" and "n", indicating the general significance of single letters as the adjudicators between truth and falsehood. Following this explanation, each part of the alphabet could be subjected to a whole host of operations.

Fazlallah and his followers made use of the *abjad* system in which letters correspond to numbers and can be manipulated through calculations to derive the connection between a text and its interpretation. The efficacy of the *abjad* system was held to have been endorsed by Muhammad himself in a hadith report that advocated learning the *abjad* and its interpretation. An example of its use is the assertion that the Quranic text can be divided into nine topics: (1) command (*amr*), (2) prohibition (*nahy*), (3) glorification and invocation (*tasbih*, *du'a*), (4) promise (*wa'ad*), (5) threat (*wa'id*), (6) stories (*qisas*, *akhbar*), (7) allowability and unlawfulness (*hall*, *hurmat*), (8) casting examples (*darb al-mithl*), and (9) abrogation (*nasikh*, *mansukh*).

According to one tabulation, the number of verses devoted to each of these topics equaled the numerical value of the letters in the title of the topic (e.g. *amr* = *a-m-r* = 1000 verses), and the total numerical value of the words used to describe these topics was 6666, the number of verses in the Qur'an. The text therefore had a complete numerical understructure, pointing both to its own perfection and the fact that numerical operations on it led to its deeper meanings.

Fazlallah and other authors also employed other schemes to distinguish between the letters and their attributes. In one categorization, the twenty-eight letters of Arabic were divided into halves of fourteen each based upon Qur'an 3: 7: "It is he who has revealed to you the book, wherein are verses clear (*muhkamat*) that are the Essence of the Book (*umm al-kitab*), and others ambiguous (*mutashabihat*)." The fourteen "clear" letters were the ones that occur in the groups of separate letters to be found in the beginnings of certain Qur'anic chapters. These were seen as the Essence of the Book, while it was shown through various processes that the remaining fourteen could be derived from them.

The clear letters could be deciphered directly as well. For example, the three letters *alif-lam-mim* found at the beginning of the second chapter (*sura*) of the Qur'an were said to refer to Allah (God), Jibra'il (Gabriel), and Muhammad. The occurrence of these letters at the beginning of the chapter was a reference to the process of revelation in which God's word had been conveyed to Muhammad through Gabriel's intermediacy. This interpretation connected the *alif-lam-mim* to the first verse of the chapter: "This is the book about which there is no doubt, a guidance for those who are pious" (Q. 2: 1).

LETTERS AND PHYSICAL REALITY

The positions of the letters in the alphabet and their physical shapes also received considerable attention in Fazlallah's movement. For example, the letter *alif* was thought to point to God because it was the first letter of both the alphabet and the name Allah, and also because the uniqueness and uprightness of its shape pointed to the singularity of God's essence. The rest of the alphabet was rationalized along similar lines so that connections were established between the letters and certain crucial terms and expressions in which they occur (e.g. *mim* for Muhammad, *lam* for Gabriel/Jibra'il, *vav* for Eve/Havva, etc.). Through a similar operation, the whole alphabet could be read as a litany containing the ninety-nine names customarily attributed to God in Islamic thought.

It was argued that all letters originated from three basic shapes: straight (*mustaqim*), rounded (*mustadir*), and bent (*mu'wajj*). These shapes were exemplified by the letters *alif*, *lam*, and *ha*, which was no accident since these three letters form the word Allah. The alphabet as a whole could thus be seen as pointing to God. The shapes of the letters corresponded directly to the parts of the human body as well, recalling the connection between speech and material reality going back to the command "be" uttered by God in the beginning of creation. Concrete examples for the parity between letters and the human body included: the rounded *ha* that looks like the human head; the *fa* that resembles the ear; and the *sad* that looks like the eye.

The human body was also seen as articulating letters through its movements. Fazlallah claimed that his knowledge included the precise rationale behind the gestures, genuflections, and compound actions that formed standard Islamic rituals. His works contain extensive discussions of every step involved in duties such as the ritual prayer (*salat*), fasting (*sawm*), obligatory almsgiving (*zakat*), and the hajj pilgrimage. The discourses on this issue get fairly convoluted but the general approach can be understood through an examination of his interpretations of the ritual prayer and fasting. He pointed out that the three characteristic postures assumed by the human body during the prayer were: standing up straight (*qiyam*), bending with hands on the knees (*ruku*'), and prostrating fully on the ground (*sujud*). These three shapes lead once again to the letters *alif*, *lam*, and *ha*, the straight, bent, and rounded letters that form the word Allah. The purpose of the postures of the prayer was therefore to articulate God's name not just through the tongue, but also physically through the body.

In a different vein, ritual fasting during Ramadan was thought to be necessary because the Qur'an had started to be revealed during this month. Fazlallah saw the Qur'an as a descent of the metalanguage in the material sphere and maintained that the process was not limited to Muhammad's lifetime but repeated every year during this particular month. The body had to be emptied of food during that month in order to make room for the letters as they descended to enter the body through the head. This same process also explained why fasting was not necessary during traveling. A body in motion could not become host to the letters anyway so that emptying it was beside the point.

Fazlallah and his followers believed that all material entities could be divided into the three shapes found in the letters. Any entity could thus be broken down into a combination of straight, bent, and rounded forms of the *alif*, *lam*, and *ha* that formed the word Allah. This proved that even though the letters of the ordinary alphabets were pale reflections of the metalinguistic alphabet, they still constituted the strongest link between apparent reality and the prototypes of materiality generated at the beginning of creation.

ABBREVIATIONS AND NEW CHARACTERS

In describing the interpretive techniques employed by Fazlallah and his followers I have so far concentrated on how they tried to connect ordinary linguistic materials to the metalanguage. There is some evidence that the "translation" from one type of language to the other worked in the opposite direction as well. The metalanguage was ordinarily beyond the purview of the outward human senses but one aspect of the textual evidence suggests that it could be made available to adepts, at least in part.

Manuscripts of works by Fazlallah Astarabadi and his followers are instantly recognizable because all the copyists used a unique alphabetic symbolism to denote certain words (see Plate 1). This occurred in two ways: first, they employed a system of abbreviation replacing frequently used terms and names with a few letters; and second, they invented new characters to refer to Fazlallah's name and the Persian words for twenty-eight and thirty-two. Most modern scholars who have examined these manuscripts have thought that this symbolism was a protective device to make the works meaningless to the uninitiated. The difficulty of deciphering this symbolism, it is argued, was meant to impede the progress of those inclined to charge Fazlallah's followers with heresy. It is difficult to assess this possibility in full because we know exceedingly little about the social life of the early communities of followers. However, the special symbolism seems to indicate something more than just the desire to confound the movement's critics.

Fazlallah's major aim in propagating his views was to inform the world about the dawn of a new dispensation, and an open proclamation of the message was clearly part of his agenda. The distinctive textual symbolism is utilized in all surviving manuscripts, of which the earliest is dated 845/1441–42. It is

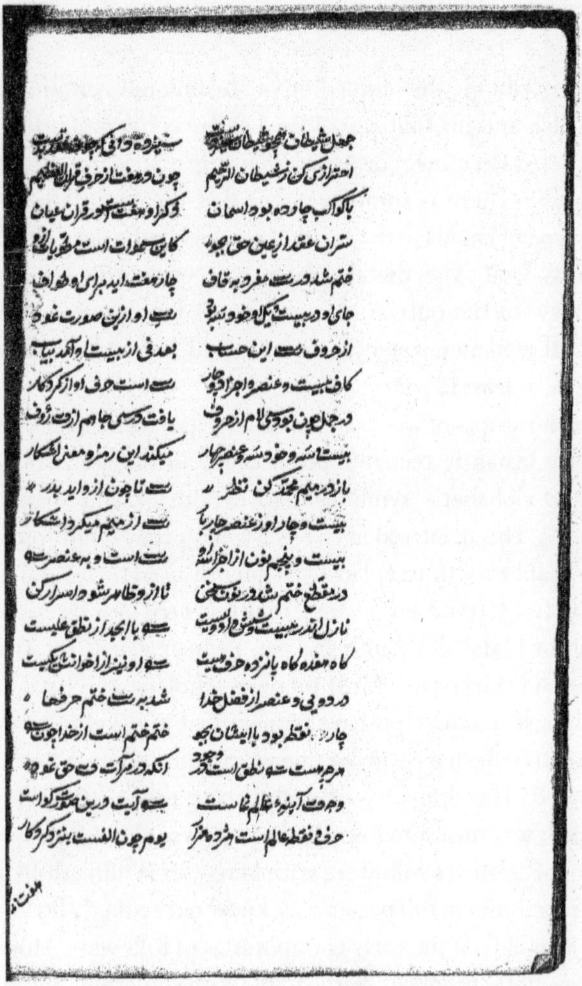

Plate 1. A page from ‘Ali al-A‘la’s *Book of the Divine Footstool* (*Kursinama*), MS. Persan 255, Bibliothèque Nationale, Paris, fol. 136b. The new characters used in Hurufi manuscripts can be seen as follows: (i) Character for twenty-eight (*bist-o-hasht*) – lines 5, 6, 7, 8, 11, 12, 13, 17; (ii) Character for thirty-two (*si-o-du*) – lines 15, 16, 18, 19, 20; (iii) Character for Fazlallah Astarabadi (modified form of the regular letter *fay*) – line 9.

impossible to pinpoint the exact moment the system was generated since most manuscripts are undated. The symbolism makes the manuscripts stand out rather than making them inconspicuous and some manuscripts even contain glossaries explaining the abbreviations and symbols for the reader's benefit. The argument that the symbolism was a device aimed at self-preservation is plausible for the case of ordinary people looking to condemn the movement. Such readers would have found the manuscripts largely unintelligible and would have had little to go on to make a case for heresy. However, the difficulty of understanding introduced through the use of the symbolism could not have afforded much protection from learned critics since even modern readers of the texts such as myself have little difficulty deciphering the symbols from their contexts. A scholar trained in the medieval Islamic academic style would, therefore, have been able to see through the abbreviations quite easily.

I would like to suggest that the special symbolism intended more than just protection from stray criticism. This opinion is based on the fact that the names and concepts given in special code were hardly the ones most problematic from the point of view of Islamic orthodoxy. They were also not aimed at hiding the movement's critical opinions about other Muslim groups that may have been seen as enemies. In fact, the codes referred only to terms most significant for Fazlallah's own theoretical system, and within the codes, the new characters were reserved for the most elevated and central concepts of Fazlallah's religion. Thus, the texts contained abbreviations for Adam, Eve, Gabriel, Jesus, Muhammad, etc., and entirely new characters represented Fazlallah himself and the numbers at the roots of his speculations on the letters (twenty-eight and thirty-two). The character for Fazlallah's name was particularly significant in this regard since it provided a single letter for the multiple meanings associated with both his name and his person. It signified, in one instantaneous visual moment: the literal meaning of the name (God's grace), Fazlallah as a historical person, and his status as God's most explicit manifestation in terrestrial form. Works by Fazlallah's disciples were deliberately written so that the term would connote all three of these significations. The availability of a single character likely made the necessarily intertwined meanings of the term even more explicit to the initiated reader.

My view is that, rather than being a mere disguise for their religious ideas, the movement's new textual symbolism was an effort to translate the metalanguage directly into the material sphere. The new symbolism was in part a new alphabet that had a closer connection to the abstract metalanguage. On this issue, it is also significant to note that Fazlallah wrote his longest work, *The Great Book of Eternal Life* (*Javidannama-yi kabir*), in the obscure Astarabadi dialect of Persian. He was highly proficient in standard Persian and wrote in that language as well, including a smaller redaction of the *Book of Eternal Life*. The choice of Astarabadi dialect over standard Persian resonates with his general theory about languages superseding each other through newer scriptures. The Astarabadi dialect was Fazlallah's native tongue, and his writing in it reflected the fact that it was to be seen as the materialized language closest to the metalanguage.

By accepting Fazlallah's science of letters, humans were expected to guarantee their salvation on the eve of the apocalypse and final destruction of the world. The new symbolism was the most obvious form of the science, and it transcended earlier alphabets in the same way that Fazlallah and his discourse superseded earlier prophets and their scriptures. To inscribe the new characters on paper was to show one's acceptance of Fazlallah's overall system. It was, furthermore, to mark oneself as a member of an elect group that possessed direct access to divine knowledge as embodied in the letters of the metalanguage.

THE WAGES OF APOCALYPTICISM

Behind all the speculation on sounds, letters, and words discussed in this chapter lies eventually the fact that Fazlallah saw his own physical body as a receptacle for the thirty-two metalinguistic letters. These had descended on him during his enlightenment and enabled him to both see himself in all of creation and project his power through all time and space. Infused with the metalanguage, he was the real Adam, formed in God's image and endowed with all his essential attributes. He was thus the progenitor of all prophets, saints, and other humans, and they were obligated to prostrate in front of him in recognition of his unmatched status. The incorporation of all forms and knowledges in his person meant that his coming denoted the Gathering (*mahshar*) of all beings that precedes the Day of Judgment in Islamic eschatology. Those who refused to accept Fazlallah as the repository of the cosmos and a direct reflection of God's essence prior to the physical apocalypse were condemned to a death of ignorance followed by eternal damnation.

The centrality of the apocalyptic message in Fazlallah's movement is explained evocatively in an anonymous text named *The Book of the Messiah* (*Masihnama*). The author of this work assigns a particular significance to the Black Stone that is affixed to the Ka'ba in Mecca and has been central to Muslims' pilgrimage experience from Muhammad's time to the present day. He states that, according to a hadith report, at the time of apocalypse the Black Stone will break open to reveal two eyes and a tongue, mimicking the form of the human face. It will then vocalize the word "yes" (*bala*) that the Qur'an reports was uttered by all human souls in the beginning of time when God had asked them the question, "Am I not your Lord?" (7: 172). This "yes" articulated by a stone turned into a human face was to be seen as the cosmic equivalent of the eighth line of the human face discussed in Chapter 4. While material reality in the form of the Black Stone was going to speak, quite literally, at the time of the physical apocalypse, those who knew Fazlallah's science of letters could already see the cosmos as a speaking/writing entity using the techniques employed in his works. The cosmos had in fact always been speaking and writing but this activity was visible only to those who understood the metalanguage. Once the apocalypse came, material existence would appear as text and sound to everyone in the most literal sense.

Human beings alive in Fazlallah's times were witnessing the beginning of the process of the apocalypse and resurrection. The choices they faced at that moment are summarized in the following lengthy excerpt from an anonymous text named *The Book of Advice* (*Hidayatnama*) written by one of Fazlallah's followers:

> God has said in the Qur'an that one indication of the day of resurrection is that smoke will descend from the sky: "a day when the sky will produce a manifest smoke" (44: 10). This 'manifest smoke' is the unveiling of the [metalinguistic] letters and the science of letters. Letters can be likened to smoke because they themselves and the science of letters exhibit their forms in black lines. This is so both in the divine realm – in the case of the creative pen and the way God wrote on the faces of Adam and his descendants – and in the created realm, where people write on paper and in notebooks. That God meant letters when he said smoke is proven from 'Ali's saying that

> smoke will descend from heaven before the day of resurrection and will enter the unbelievers' ears to turn their heads into heads of *hayna'idhin*, which means the roasted head of a calf. For the believers (in comparison), the smoke will induce a condition resembling the common cold ... Smoke usually affects eyes and not ears, but these are letters that enter the ears of the unjust and the tradition-bound (*muqalladan*). They hear them but their great envy compels them not to embrace them. They remain unbelievers as a result of this and their heads become ... like roasted heads of animals incapable of utilizing the letters ... The believers attract a cold (from the letters) since a cold cleanses the brain from constricting and impure substances ... When the smoke of letters enters the ears of the believers, their brains are cleansed of impure and confusing traditional notions and non-existent imaginations regarding the Return (*ma'ad*) and the End (*akhirat*). Then, once physical death destroys their bodies, they find themselves in the highest paradise as a reward for having stopped following (the religion of) their parents blindly and acquiring true apprehensions from a perfected guide. They dwell in it for eternity, never again tasting death, sitting on grand thrones in well-constructed forms, possessing the ability to see God, served by female and male pages (*huris* and *ghulams*), completely free of dissension and veils, pains and jealousies, having achieved all that a soul desires and presented with all that is savory to the eye.

While this statement connects to Fazlallah's theories in a number of different ways, its most remarkable aspect is the description of a physical reaction between the letters descending from the sky and damned and saved human beings. For the author, the letters were descending at that moment since the end time had arrived, and what mattered most was to prepare one's body so that it became a welcoming receptacle for them. Those who rejected Fazlallah's message were forsaking the path of salvation and their bodies were turning into those of dead animals.

Such beings were damned and were, like animals, incapable of receiving the reward God has promised for the next life. The bodies of Fazlallah's followers, on the other hand, were becoming sanctified in anticipation of the time when their redeemed souls would depart from them and reside in bliss for eternity.

The only way to bring oneself in line with the times was to accept Fazlallah's vision and become his follower. By mentally recognizing the truth, an individual could transform his or her own body into one like that of Fazlallah, representing perfect harmony between materiality and language. At least for those who were alive at the time, the physical bodies they possessed were their passports on the imminent Day of Judgment. A proper understanding of the metalanguage and the science of letters led one to ultimate knowledge and its corollaries, eternal salvation and bliss. Descendants of Adam who were able to accomplish this eliminated the estrangement between materiality and sound instituted at the dawn of creation. As a result, such beings fulfilled the purpose of the creation of the cosmos by knowing God and coming to sit in front of him in the divine court. Given the comprehensiveness and promise of Fazlallah's system, it is no surprise that the community of his followers were faced with a tremendous crisis when he was arrested and executed before they had witnessed the realization of his vision.

6

SHRINE AND SUCCESSORS

Fazlallah Astarabadi's death in Zu l-Qa'da 796 (September 1394) came as a huge shock to his followers. An elegy by 'Ali al-A'la, a prominent disciple, states that people's faces turned white when they heard the news and some were completely besides themselves with grief. It is understandable that a community centered round a charismatic leader would have been stricken by his unexpected demise. Moreover, as the previous two chapters have shown, Fazlallah was much more than a human leader for his followers. They saw him as the apex of their cosmological hierarchy and the consummation of all historical processes, a fulfillment of the very desire that had compelled God to create the cosmos. Fazlallah's intellectual system had put a tremendous emphasis on the human body and the material cosmos as the ultimate loci for God's manifestation. His lifeless and mutilated body lying in front of his followers represented not just the demise of their hopes but also a fundamental challenge to their whole worldview.

Historical and social scientific studies have shown that prophetic and apocalyptic religious movements almost never crumble when their expectations are abruptly shown to be untenable. They usually see the new circumstances as having been preordained and get to the task of developing a new program of action. Following this pattern, Fazlallah's followers did not see his death as the end of their religious system either. Instead, they immediately began the task of reinterpreting the system to make sense of the unforeseen event. They felt that, like Fazlallah's life, his death must have cosmological meaning and that this could be derived from examining what he had done and written before his death. The process of reinterpretation split the group into factions with differing views. Some felt that what Fazlallah had provided was enough to prepare them for the impending apocalypse while others thought that he would have a second coming. Fazlallah's major disciples and some of his children led these factions during the fifteenth century. Later generations of the movement's leaders became increasingly distant from Fazlallah's apocalyptic ideas and, by the end of the fifteenth century, all that was left of Fazlallah's vision was the movement's literature.

During the period when Fazlallah's movement retained its social vitality, the shrine constructed over his place of burial in Alinjaq became its symbolic center. The movement attracted substantial numbers of followers in Iran, Central Asia, and Anatolia, who made pilgrimages to the shrine and expected that it would become the starting point of the apocalypse about to unfold in their view. Seen as a substitute for Fazlallah's physical presence, the shrine was also invested with much of the cosmological significance that they had attached to Fazlallah's body during his life.

THE SHRINE

Like other aspects of Fazlallah's history, we know of his shrine only through oblique references in the movement's literature. Some reports concerning his execution state that the dead body was dragged through the streets or even burned. In spite of possible mutilation, it was eventually delivered to his followers who conducted a funeral and buried it. Our only information about the day to day functioning of the shrine constructed over the grave comes from certain verses in 'Ali al-A'la's *Book of the Divine Footstool* (*Kursinama*), completed in 810/1407, where a man named Musa is named as its caretaker. From the same source, we can tell that the shrine became dilapidated and was reconstructed by some of Fazlallah's devout followers either six or fourteen years after the initial burial.

While we have no physical description of the shrine, we can surmise its shape and the underlying architectural principle from its uses and the place it occupied in the movement's cosmology. Most significantly, Fazlallah's followers believed that the shrine replaced the Ka'ba in Mecca as the center of Islam since it was the final abode of the incarnated divine being. In accordance with the general principle of Fazlallah's religious system, the shrine was declared the "true Ka'ba" and the older house of God as a mere symbol of it. Just as Fazlallah had exteriorized the hidden truth of Islam through his knowledge of the divine metalanguage, so the new Ka'ba superseded the older one as the truer center of the universe that could have been made visible only at the end of time. All heavenly bodies and angels were seen to prostrate in its direction and, in the human sphere, the symbolism and rituals attached to the old Ka'ba were shifted to the shrine. Fazlallah's followers now performed the smaller pilgrimage (*'umra*) as well as the hajj around it in a pattern taken over in a slightly altered form from normative Islamic practice.

The mainstream hajj is performed during the first half of Zu l-Hijja, the twelfth month of the Islamic calendar. The new hajj took place in the month of Zu l-Qa'da, the eleventh month, and culminated on the fifteenth day. The participants were required to put on the pilgrims' clothes required for the normative hajj: two large pieces of unstitched cloth for men and plain versions of normal dress for women. The major ritual was circumambulations of the shrine in multiples of seven. Emulating the stoning of Satan in the Meccan ritual, the last rite of the new hajj included three successive occasions where pilgrims cast twenty-one stones at the nearby castle of Sanjariyya, identified as the home of Miranshah, Fazlallah's executioner. Works written by Fazlallah's followers after his death contain numerous exhortations to the community to visit the shrine, indicating that the ritual was central to the community's identity.

In his works, Fazlallah provided extensive rationalizations for the physical actions undertaken during Islamic ritual prayer (*salat*), fasting, the hajj, and other normative rituals. Along the same lines, his followers now gave the rites of the new hajj elaborate justifications that made the ritual acts understandable in ordinary terms. They claimed that the four walls of the Ka'ba's square shape represented the elements earth, wind, fire, and water that formed the physical universe. The set of seven circumambulations were performed four times (once for each wall/element) and the total came to twenty-eight, the number of letters in the Arabic alphabet. The seven circumambulations themselves referred to the seven levels of meaning that were thought to lie underneath all symbols. Similarly, Miranshah's castle was stoned only three times with seven stones – once each for the three elements earth, water, and wind – since he himself represented fire in the form of Satan. The interpretation of these rituals exemplified the perfect internal symmetry of the cosmos first revealed to Fazlallah during his lifetime. Knowledge of this symmetry was within human understanding as long as one knew the connections between the metalanguage on the one hand and ordinary languages and physical reality on the other.

Along with its ritual usage, Fazlallah's followers incorporated the shrine in their cosmology based on Fazlallah's idea that God had formed Adam's face from the clay of Mecca (i.e. Alinjaq, the true Ka'ba). Since Adam had been formed in God's image and had been given God's knowledge in the form of the alphabet of the metalanguage, the clay of Mecca was seen as the greatest material recipient of God's self-disclosure. The interment of Fazlallah's body into the earth of Alinjaq was a reversal of the process that had initiated the human species. At the culmination of the process of creation, Adam's body had been formed from a lump of clay separated from the earth of Alinjaq. At the time of the apocalypse, when creation was about to be folded, the lump of material substances represented by Fazlallah's body was returned to the same spot. Adam and Fazlallah were thus seen, respectively, as the beginning and the end of the lifespan of the human species.

As discussed in previous chapters, Fazlallah believed that the perfection of the human face was carried forth through history in the form of human discourse. This applied to both speech, vocalized through the human mouth, and the written word formed by combining letters, creation's primordial symbols. As the end of the cosmos approached, Fazlallah's followers felt that eschatological realities were also reflected in the human face. The seven openings of the face (two ears, eyes, and nostrils each, and the mouth) were thus equated with the conventionally accepted seven doors of paradise. Since it was the apogee of the process of creation, the face was seen also as the "farthest lote-tree" (*sidrat-i muntaha*) near which Muhammad saw God (or an angel) according to a Qur'anic account (53: 14). Accession to heaven at the end of time was therefore a kind of return to the perfection of Adam's face whose potential was inherent in every human being. The burial of Fazlallah's body at

Alinjaq was the beginning of the whole process of "return" to the origins at the end of time. The shrine at Alinjaq was thus a metonymic marker for the impending apocalypse.

In summary, Fazlallah's shrine at Alinjaq was crucial to his followers' rituals and ideology. As the site of the yearly hajj, it functioned (or at least was meant to function) as the most significant attempt to draw the community together after his demise. In addition, it was seen as the source of the human being; travel to it was the equivalent of a return to the place of one's origin. While God's creation of Adam in his own image had begun the connection between divinity and humanity, Fazlallah's body, interred in the shrine at Alinjaq, most fully and explicitly realized the potential divinity within all humans. The shrine was, therefore, the earthly home of God, the source of Adam, and the point of eventual return for the righteous all rolled up into one. In Fazlallah's system the cosmos was an organic whole in which one's ability to interpret one "system," such as the alphabet or the human face, enabled one to understand other "systems," such as hidden matters like life after death. The shrine was the most concrete representation of this complex ontological unity since it literally and metaphorically contained Fazlallah's being.

A SPLIT COMMUNITY

As discussed in previous chapters, Fazlallah's followers regarded him as both an embodiment of divinity and the deliverer who was to save humanity at the end of time as predicted in messianic traditions. His followers maintained their apocalyptic beliefs in the first few decades after his execution, though how the apocalypse was to be seen was a matter of contention between two factions. Fazlallah had himself divided the apocalypse into two phases: the first was his own enlightenment, when the veil had been lifted from the physical world, and the second was to be the cataclysmic destruction of the material sphere. After his death, one group of his followers believed that the first phase had in fact been the full apocalypse. A second group thought that he had only begun his work in the first life and would come back in the near future to lead them to a universal victory before the dissolution of the cosmos.

The eschatological apocalypse was, for all of Fazlallah's followers, a revelation of the mystery underlying the cosmos. They believed that God had pledged exactly such a momentous revelation for the end times, and that the science of letters that could be learnt from Fazlallah's works fulfilled this promise. Fazlallah's knowledge and the circumstances of his life were the signs heralding the messiah's appearance and the end of time. The events of his life were also the fulfillment of well-known sayings by Muhammad, including the one that states that paradise lies under mothers' feet. By "mothers" Muhammad had meant the fourteen unexplained letters found in the beginning of some chapters in the Qur'an that Fazlallah equated with the "clear" revelations. The true meaning of these letters lay under them, so that those who acquired the science of letters by heeding Fazlallah's revelation drew close to the ultimate bliss of paradise.

The difference of opinion between Fazlallah's followers was really about the promised accession to paradise. Those who equated the first phase with the full apocalypse thought that knowing Fazlallah's science had already put them in paradise, while those who expected him to return also expected more cosmic events to occur prior to the realization of paradisiacal joys. The former viewpoint, reportedly popular among some believers in Rum, Iraq, Kurdistan, Shirvan, Gilan and Azerbaijan, stated that:

> Paradise and hell are, in essence, representations of knowledge and ignorance, respectively. Since we are cognizant of the thirty-two letters, of our own being, and of all things, all things are paradise to us. Actions such as ritual prayer, fasting, and cleanliness, and the differentiation between that which is religiously lawful and unlawful, are no longer incumbent upon us. These matters are all obligations that have no place in paradise. Paradise is the world that surrounds us, except with knowledge of the science of letters and the explanations of the Master of Esoteric Interpretation (i.e. Fazlallah).

Our knowledge of the full beliefs of this group is limited to what is reported in works written by the opposition. The fact that none of the written sources contains a defense of this position suggests that this view was popular among followers whose religious worldview was tied to the new mode of action prescribed for human beings rather than theoretical rationalization. Those who feel that they are already in paradise after a final judgment have, in any case, little reason to explain their condition for the benefit of others.

In contrast with the metaphorical entry into paradise offered by the ideas of this group, others believed that paradise and hell were real places, populated by inhabitants appropriate for each. The author who documents the controversy states that one night he saw in a dream four of Fazlallah's children who had perished in a plague in 1417–18. They told him that they were in heaven and it was exactly the way it had been described in the Qur'an. To prove their point, they took him on a tour so that he could see for himself things such as rivers, shady fruit-laden trees, colorful flowers, and houses filled with silken fabrics. In keeping with Fazlallah's teachings and experiences, his followers regarded the events of this dream as true occurrences since what one saw in dreams was the measure of one's fate in the afterlife. The opposing group accepted this viewpoint based upon Fazlallah's teachings, but argued that dreams had ceased to function in this way since Fazlallah's death. In other words, heaven and hell had already been "filled" with those who had, respectively, accepted or rejected Fazlallah's revelation: afterlife had already begun, and one's dreams no longer served as an indication of what was to come in this respect.

Those who did not think themselves to be in paradise supported the continued observance of rituals. They contended that acts of devotion were praiseworthy in all circumstances since they were expressions of love toward the divine being. 'Ali al-A'la countered the idea that ritual requirements had lapsed by recalling a hadith that states that prayers are the talk of the heavens and are performed even in paradise. Furthermore, echoing Fazlallah's own perspective, he stated that the movement of the head and body during prayers was the equivalent of vocalizing words written through the combination of letters. The human body and the letters of the alphabet were derived from God's essence and these came "alive" through the act of prayer or vocalization respectively. Another author stated that rituals were an aspect of the love that connected humanity and divinity. He explained that human beings' belief that they loved God when they embarked upon a religious path was a mere illusion. The truth was that it was God who was the active lover since the human being was God's beloved. An individual seeker came to recognize this truth only when s/he understood the esoteric doctrines explained in Fazlallah's works.

THE SECOND COMING

The difference of opinion between the Hurufis went beyond matters of doctrine since the two perspectives had varying implications for human action at the societal level. Some who believed that they were in paradise took the idea further by stating that they had the right to the lives and property of those outside the group. They declared: "Whatever is in creation is the right of the knowledgeable person. He should procure and utilize everything obtainable to him, and, for things beyond his reach, regard them as his right and strive to get them out of others' hands." The suffering caused to the unconverted from any such activity was, presumably, justifiable since they were in hell and deserved punishment. The faith of the paradise-dwellers provided them a license to satisfy their desires, though we have no evidence that they acted upon this conviction to create social unrest.

Against this view, those who did not believe themselves to be in paradise, began to wait for Fazlallah's return after his death. They expected him to avenge his death in the first life and create a just society prior to the total destruction of the physical world. Taking their cues from Fazlallah's own pronouncements, they now began to scrutinize events surrounding them in order to find hints about the messiah's resurrection.

The cryptic evidence for the exact beliefs of this group comes from 'Ali al-A'la's versified *Book of the Divine Footstool* and we can be sure that, as the new house of God, the shrine at Alinjaq and its geographical context were at the very center of the expectation. This group concentrated on three common prophetic traditions about the messiah, which stated that he would (1) raise the flag of rebellion in Khurasan, (2) acquire the allegiance of a party of the righteous in Mecca, and (3) conquer the city of Constantinople. They thus expected Fazlallah to begin his movement in Khurasan and then travel westward to

Shirvan and Azerbaijan. Fazlallah's first birth in Astarabad (an area included in Khurasan) and his enlightenment in Azerbaijan were taken as preambles to his activity in the second coming. The oath of allegiance to the messiah was to occur at Alinjaq, the new Ka'ba, where Fazlallah was to be united with his erstwhile followers. He was then expected to progress westward, eventually conquering Constantinople, still the capital of the Byzantine empire. This city did fall to the Muslim Ottomans in 1453, though we have no information about what members of Fazlallah's movement made of this event. Paralleling the shifts that underlay Fazlallah's ideology and the construction of the Alinjaq shrine, they moved the Islamic messianic expectation from an Arabia-centered normative Islam to the Azerbaijan-centered new version.

'Ali al-A'la's *Book of the Divine Footstool* also provides the only direct indication of an effort to fix a time for Fazlallah's second coming, in the form of an interpretation of certain Qur'anic verses that had other uses in the intellectual system as well. The text in question was Qur'an 30: 2–4: "The Byzantines have been vanquished in the nearer part of the land; and, after their vanquishing, they shall be the victors in a few (*bid'*) years. To God belongs the command before and after, and on that day the believers shall rejoice in God's help." As discussed in Chapter 5, one author interpreted this text to signify the creation of Adam and Eve. It was given an entirely different meaning in the context of the speculation about Fazlallah's second coming. This was not a problem since all Qur'anic texts were thought to have seven different levels of meaning.

'Ali al-A'la's understanding of this Qur'anic text is reflected in the following verses:

> The source of all will indeed become apparent at the time of
> the 'few' (*bid'*)

Understand the appearance of God's grace (*fazl-i haqq*) to be
the seeds the farmer spread on the earth
On that day, the believers will rejoice in God's aid and the
infidels will be in distress

These verses likened Fazlallah's first coming to the work of a farmer who prepares the ground for an eventual harvest. The prediction of the believers' "rejoicing" in the Qur'anic text was transposed to the fortunes of Fazlallah's community, and the "nearer part of the land" was taken to be Azerbaijan. The word "few" (*bid*') was crucial in this interpretation since its numerical value in the *abjad* system, 830, was seen as the year in which Fazlallah would come back to the earth to complete his messianic mission. The Muslim year 830 corresponds to the end of the Christian year 1426 and the beginning of 1427. It is impossible to judge whether this year had received general acceptance by the movement's adherents or if it was only one possibility being discussed among many others.

Regardless of exact predictions, many of Fazlallah's followers alive in the beginning of the fifteenth century clearly did consider his return to be imminent within their lifetimes. To this end, they readied themselves for a struggle, waiting for the time when Fazlallah would reach Baku, in Azerbaijan, and issue a call for his supporters to join him. The community thus retained the aspirations to political success that Fazlallah himself had harbored. The Timurids were the community's natural enemies since Timur had ordered Fazlallah's execution and his son Miranshah had carried it out. Works by Fazlallah's followers written in this period consistently demonized Miranshah as the Dajjal, the Islamic antichrist figure. Focusing once again on bodily indicators, they pointed particularly to the fact that Miranshah had an extremely hairy face that, unlike other human faces, did not have seven clear hairlines. The Timurids were equated with the hordes of Gog and Magog as well, who are supposed to flood the earth before the apocalypse. The community's tense relationship with the rulers meant that the propagation of the movement had to be carried out through clandestine means.

MAJOR DISCIPLES

Fazlallah's execution marked his followers as a subversive group that could not openly carry out its mandate to spread Fazlallah's apocalyptic message. Consequently, sources from the period provide very few concrete details about their activities. The movement's continuing vitality in the decades following Fazlallah's death can be gauged only from the very substantial surviving literature produced by his followers. Although Fazlallah's children were the bearers of his charisma, relatively little is known about them; they seem not to have authored any works and none of the other authors provide details about their lives and views. However, Fazlallah's intellectual and social perspective attracted a significant band of talented and well-trained individuals who clarified or elaborated on his ideas and carried the message further than the geographical regions where Fazlallah had himself been active. One can get a sense of the characteristics of the movement's nucleus by considering three men with differing personalities and writing styles.

ʻAli al-Aʻla (d. 1419) was, in hindsight, Fazlallah's most influential disciple, although he was by no means the sole chosen successor. We know very little for certain about his life. His reputation as a major propagator of Fazlallah's movement rests on two facts: his considerable literary output and the claim of the Bektashis (whose belief system includes some of

Fazlallah's ideas) that 'Ali al-A'la was the missionary who brought the material to them. 'Ali al-A'la's works are almost all narrative poetry and illuminate both Fazlallah's ideology and the circumstances of Fazlallah's life. The historical references make it clear that 'Ali al-A'la was close to Fazlallah during his lifetime and was present at the time when Fazlallah's body was handed over to the community after the execution. His own works contain references to the expectation of the second coming and one of his disciples and nephews writes that he was Fazlallah's greatest successor and opposed the faction that believed that paradise was already at hand after Fazlallah's death.

Besides participating in internal discussions, 'Ali al-A'la traveled westward from Iran to gain converts to Fazlallah's ideology. His works and reports by one of his disciples mention Syria and localities in Anatolia (e.g. Aladagh, near present-day Adana, Turkey) as places to which he traveled and where he engaged in religious disputation. The sole indication of Fazlallah's ideas receiving attention in Syria and Egypt is the poetry of the Sultan Qansuh al-Ghuri (d. 1516), which contains references to the alphabet. Anatolia in the fifteenth century was increasingly becoming dominated by the Ottoman dynasty. 'Ali al-A'la's status as the person who introduced Fazlallah to Ottoman domains rests on three points: the mention of Anatolia in his own works; the fact the Bektashi order saw him as the missionary of Fazlallah's movement to them; and the fact that he is condemned as a heretical influence on the Bektashis by Ottoman authors opposed to the order. This is clearly too little to give a clear picture of his activity. About the best that can be inferred is that he was in fact active in Anatolia. Sources internal to the movement place his death in 1419 and state that he was buried next to Fazlallah in Alinjaq. While some sources state that 'Ali al-A'la was also executed, the internal tradition does not represent him as a martyr. He very likely returned to the movement's central shrine after his missionary travels and died of natural causes.

Like 'Ali al-A'la, Khwaja Sayyid Ishaq was also a faithful companion to Fazlallah during his life and a propagandist for the cause after his death. He was the author of numerous works in prose and poetry that inform about Fazlallah's life and dream interpretations, and clarify the religious theses presented in Fazlallah's works. Some of Khwaja Ishaq's works are written in the Astarabadi dialect, indicating that he shared a regional identity with the movement's founder. In a work written after Fazlallah's execution, Khwaja Ishaq mentions seeing Fazlallah in a dream during a visit to the grave of Abu Muslim Khurasani (d. 755). Abu Muslim was a military commander with Shi'i sympathies who helped bring about the rise of the 'Abbasid dynasty in early Islamic history. He was perceived to be a threat soon after the 'Abbasid revolution (750) and was executed by the very people he had helped bring to power. In subsequent centuries, Abu Muslim became a legendary figure for groups that stressed a combination of Shi'ism and Persian ethnic and linguistic identity within the Islamic world. Khwaja Ishaq's mentioning Abu Muslim indicates that he may have been particularly attracted to Fazlallah's system because of his high regard for Persian ethnicity. His activities after Fazlallah's death were concentrated in the Khurasan region and his preeminence in the movement is reflected in the title Pir-i Khurasan (The Elder of Khurasan).

Khwaja Ishaq's works have, on the whole, a more militant voice than those of 'Ali al-A'la. Besides glorifying Fazlallah, he criticizes the movement's detractors very severely although, curiously, he mentions Timur in positive terms. Apparently, not all of Fazlallah's followers were against the Timurid state. Some at least saw the tragedies that had befallen their movement as a result of actions taken at the local level. For such followers,

Fazlallah's death had been the action of the Timurid governor Miranshah, undertaken on the behest of the petty overlord of Shirvan, the region where Fazlallah was arrested. One interesting fact we learn from Khwaja Ishaq's works is that he regarded Fazlallah's daughter Kalimatallah al-'Ulya as the founder's principal heir. The fact that this daughter does not figure prominently in the works of other disciples suggests that the community did not rally around a single leader in the decades after Fazlallah's death. Khwaja Ishaq's allegiance to one of Fazlallah's daughters may indicate a Shi'i perspective since this sect of Islam bases itself on the rights of generations descended from Muhammad's daughter Fatima. Surviving sources do not provide any details about the year or circumstances of Khwaja Ishaq's death.

Of all of Fazlallah's followers, Sayyid 'Imad al-Din Nesimi (d. 1404–5) garnered the greatest fame. His celebrity rested on his Turkic and Persian poetry which shows deep knowledge of Islamic poetic traditions as well as a genius for composition in the lyrical and quatrain forms. Nesimi is among the very few followers mentioned in Fazlallah's own works, indicating that he must have impressed Fazlallah through personal contact. His poetry contains frequent mentions of Fazlallah as the guide and the messiah and also elucidates many religious themes found in Fazlallah's works. His tremendous affection and regard for Fazlallah, to which there are parallels in the works of other authors, is evident in the following Turkic quatrain:

> The Grace of the Lord (*fazl-i rabb*), possessor of majesty,
> he was for us
> Goodness and beauty and comeliness he was for us
> Our father, endowed with excellence, he was for us
> Our mother, his milk sanctified, he was for us

All that can be said for certain about Nesimi's life is that he came from a Turkic background and traveled extensively in the period after Fazlallah's death. His poetry shows considerable knowledge of Islamic, particularly Sufi, religious ideas, indicating that he must have had religious training besides that required for assimilation of Fazlallah's system. His gift as a poet was instrumental in conveying Fazlallah's ideas to the Turkish-speaking population of Anatolia. He traveled extensively and was executed on a charge of heresy in Aleppo, Syria, in 1404–5. The circumstances of his death are not fully clear though it seems to have resulted from a combination of religious and political factors. His passionate poetry, which extols Fazlallah as well as earlier Sufi figures like Hallaj, would have raised eyebrows in the religious establishment. The fact that the Mamluk rulers of Syria gave orders for his execution (and possible flaying) suggests that his religious views may have attracted a substantial following, giving rise to fears of sedition. If so, Nesimi's fate paralleled Fazlallah's own. Nesimi's poetry remained popular among speakers of Turkish in particular in later centuries but orthodox compilers of dictionaries of poets usually omitted his allegiance to Fazlallah's ideas in their entries on him. Instead, they portrayed him as a great poet and a Sufi who, like the well-known Abu Mansur al-Hallaj (d. 922) before him, was executed because of his proclamation that he had reached ecstatic union with God.

ATTACK ON MIRZA SHAHRUKH (1427)

Besides the activities of individual disciples, Fazlallah's followers as a group were implicated in a number of political incidents during the fifteenth century. There is no indication that the movement had any central organization or acted with a coordinated plan. Small cells operated on their own, though everyone associated with Fazlallah's teachings faced imprisonment and repression following any political strike.

In one case of noteworthy political involvement, the Timurid ruler Shahrukh (d. 1447) was attacked with a knife. This took place on Friday, 23 Rabi' II, 830 (21 February 1427) in Herat and the attacker was a man named Ahmad-i Lur. The king was grievously injured but not killed, and his guards put the assailant to death straightaway. A search of his clothing produced a key that led officials to his dwellings in the bazaar. It was then discovered that he was a member of a seditious group of Fazlallah's followers made up of the city's drapers, tailors, and capmakers who had been busy brewing a revolt in the city. A famous calligrapher named Mawlana Ma'ruf was implicated in the matter who eventually confessed to a conspiracy which led to the arrest of a whole group.

Deeper investigation into the matter revealed that Ahmad-i Lur had arrived in Herat recently from Shirvan, the region where Fazlallah had been arrested. It is quite possible that the timing of the attack correlated with the Hurufis' expectations of Fazlallah's second coming. As discussed above, 'Ali al-A'la's *Book of the Divine Footstool* names the year 830 (1426–27 CE), which corresponds with the numerical value of the word *bid'* (few) in Qur'an 30: 4, as the year for this event. Ahmad-i Lur and his companions may have thought that the act of killing the king would begin the series of events leading to Fazlallah's reappearance and, eventually, the apocalypse.

The authorities imprisoned Mawlana Ma'ruf, their key informant, and then proceeded to execute and burn a number of Hurufis, including Fazlallah's maternal grandson 'Azud al-Din Astarabadi. Following the incident, a prominent scholar named Sa'in al-Din Turka (d. 1432–33) was imprisoned and tortured and the famous Sufi poet Shah Qasim-i Anvar

(d. 1433) was forced to abandon Herat for Samarqand on suspicion of sympathizing with the Hurufis.

In the aftermath of the attempt on Shahrukh's life, one of Fazlallah's sons named Amir Nurallah was arrested and questioned in Timurid princely courts in an effort to connect him to the intrigue. A letter written by Ghiyas al-Din Astarabadi, a companion of Nurallah and the author of an important work named *The Book of the Sitting* (*Istivanama*), describes how they were both arrested in Mazandaran and taken in front of Timurid army commanders involved in a large-scale military operation being undertaken in the region against local rulers. The officials first tried to prove that Nurallah had ordered Ahmad-i Lur to carry out the attack on Shahrukh but failed to produce any concrete link. They then tried to pin on him a general charge of sedition, which also could not be confirmed. Scholars in the pay of Shahrukh then engaged him in a religious debate to prove that he held corrupt religious beliefs and deserved death. On this score too the Timurids' retainers were unable to make a convincing argument, though we have to take the report with caution given its source. The letter states that the audience found his rational explanations of Islamic rituals, like the reasoning behind the number of cycles of prayer, particularly impressive. When questioned directly about his creed, he responded that he followed the Sunni Shafi'i legal school.

It is interesting that, during his questioning by Shahrukh's courtiers, Nurallah denied the idea that Fazlallah was Jesus and would one day descend from the sky. The fact that this issue in particular was brought up once again suggests that the attack on Shahrukh may have been related to the expectation of Fazlallah's second coming in 830/1426–27. The authorities may have had partial information about this and had tried to probe Nurallah on the matter. His denial may have been pious dissimulation or, unlike Ahmad-i Lur and his companions, he may not have belonged to the party that was expecting the return at this time.

After the interrogation in Herat, the prisoners were sent to Samarqand to the court of Shahrukh's son Ulugh Beg (d. 1449), well known for his patronage of scholars and scientists. The author of the letter claims that, instead of incriminating and executing Nurallah, Ulugh Beg was intrigued by Fazlallah's ideas about language and the human body and questioned the prisoners about them at length.

The description of the intellectual discussion at Ulugh Beg's court has some concrete elements and is likely to be true at some level. The two prisoners were asked if they were materialists (i.e. people who believed the material world to be the sole existence) and Nurallah emphatically denied the suggestion. In one discussion, someone challenged the idea of thirty-two letters by stating that Chinese had six more. Nurallah's only denial of this was to cite verses by Jalal al-Din Rumi that mention the thirty-two letter alphabet. The opponent allegedly withdrew his objection because of his respect for Rumi's knowledge.

Ulugh Beg was himself a famous astronomer and asked Nurallah about his and Fazlallah's view of the stars. Nurallah began by comparing the cosmos with the microcosm of the human body and correlated the twelve constellations with the body's twelve openings. Ulugh Beg objected that the body only had nine openings: two ears, eye sockets, and nostrils each, the mouth, and the two excretory points. When Nurallah added the nipples and the belly button to these, it was objected that male nipples are never open. Nurallah stated that males do secrete milk from their nipples during infancy. There were many women present in the court who confirmed that this was true.

After these purported triumphs in Samarqand, Ulugh Beg wrote to Shahrukh that he could not punish the prisoners since he could find nothing wrong with their beliefs. The reply came that this judgment was unacceptable and Ulugh Beg eventually washed his hands of the whole affair by sending them back to Herat. They were then shuttled to various places in Iran, Iraq, and Kurdistan. The letter was written five years after the arrest (c. 836/1432–33), while they were still in captivity. Amir Nurallah was probably executed in the end since a later work by Ghiyas al-Din Astarabadi refers to him as a martyr. We do not know Ghiyas al-Din's own eventual fate.

UPRISINGS IN ISFAHAN AND TABRIZ

We have some very brief reports that a Hurufi named Hajji Surkh led a rebellion in Isfahan in 1431–32. His followers first killed two sons of an important Timurid military commander stationed in Isfahan at the time. The local garrison then hunted out the whole group and Hajji Surkh was flayed.

A slightly more detailed account is available for an incident in Tabriz in 1441–42 involving Fazlallah's daughter Kalimatallah al-'Ulya, whose son 'Azud al-Din was put to death in Herat in 1427 following the attack on Shahrukh. Kalimatallah (the name means "word of God") must have been a prominent person in the movement since, as mentioned already, Khwaja Ishaq actually names her as Fazlallah's principal heir. The sparse details on her activity indicate that she and a man named Mawlana Yusuf headed a group in Tabriz that exercised considerable influence on the Qaraqoyunlu ruler Jihan Shah (d. 1467). Fearful of their heretical beliefs, the city's scholarly establishment issued a legal opinion decrying them for heresy worthy of death. Jihan Shah resisted implementing the judgment because one major scholar, Najm al-Din Usku'i, refused to ratify it. However, Najm al-Din changed his mind after another mystic had a dream to the effect that he should go and convince Najm al-Din about the charge. Jihan Shah then had no choice and ordered the killing of Kalimatallah, Mawlana Yusuf, and five hundred of their followers in 1441–2. This bloodbath seems to have put a final end to the movement's organized activity in Azerbaijan.

ATTEMPT TO CONVERT THE OTTOMAN MEHMET THE CONQUEROR

After Kalimatallah's demise, the history of Fazlallah's movement shifts from Iran to the Ottoman empire. One propagandist for Fazlallah's ideas is reported to have tried to convert the Ottoman prince Mehmet, who later ascended the throne as Mehmet II (r. 1451–81) and became known as the Conqueror (Fatih) after wresting the city of Constantinople from the Byzantines in 1453.

The single report about this incident indicates that, around 1445, some followers of Fazlallah managed to enter Mehmet's company and made him take an interest in their doctrines. Officials in the prince's court were unhappy with this but unable to intervene directly until they enlisted the support of a scholar named Fakhr al-Din 'Ajami. The prince's vizier then invited the leader of the group to his house and pretended that he was inclined to their faith. Encouraged by this good news, he began to list all the group's doctrines, but when he reached the topic of *hulul* (the idea that divinity can reside in a human body), Fakhr al-Din could not contain himself any longer and came out to curse the "heretic" with great passion. He then pursued the offender to the palace where the latter went to seek refuge with Mehmet. However, the prince was cowed by Fakhr al-Din's ferocity and did not rise to his companion's defense. He was then taken to the new mosque in Edirne where the muezzin gave out the call for a special prayer. Once people had gathered, Fakhr al-Din denounced the group's beliefs and extolled the spiritual reward to be gained by participating in its elimination. The order was issued to prepare a fire to burn the leader of the group and extinguish the dangerous fire of this heresy before it spread. Fakhr al-Din himself became so enthusiastic in fanning the flames that his large beard caught fire. Others then put the group's leader in the fire and executed the remainder of the group by other means.

This triumphalist account comes from Fazlallah's opponents in the religious establishment, but they would hardly have dared to credit Prince Mehmet with interest in the heresy if there had not been some truth to it. Unfortunately, the account does not allow us to sense what it was that appealed to him, nor does it really tell us what was involved in the decision to suppress it. Presumably, it involved a combination of religious and political factors similar to those involved in the deaths of Fazlallah himself and Nesimi. Fazlallah clearly did see the presence of the divine in the human but he never used the term *hulul*, which has a long history of being considered heretical in Islamic thought. The propagandist put to death would not have claimed belief in *hulul* but the accusers could easily make the charge based upon the content of Fazlallah's teachings. This suppression of the movement ended any possibility of the Ottoman rulers espousing Fazlallah's ideas and, furthermore, led to Fazlallah and his followers becoming known as the archetypal heretics in later Ottoman history.

SUMMARY

After Fazlallah's death, those who believed in him were able to adjust their intellectual system to accommodate the death one way or the other. Besides reflecting on their circumstances, they remained committed to Fazlallah's apocalyptic vision and expected the world to come to an end in the near future. Many of them prepared for this eventuality by trying to enlist followers ranging from ordinary people to members of ruling houses. The stories of their endeavors end with failure but it is noteworthy that members of the movement could attract the attention of figures such as Ulugh Beg, Jihan Shah Qaraqoyunlu, and Mehmet II. Fazlallah's ideology clearly did resonate with some Muslims in this period of Islamic history.

The middle of the fifteenth century represents a significant break in the history of Fazlallah's movement. From this time onward, there are no major reports of groups undertaking political or social action in the name of his system. Fazlallah's ideas continued to interest and inspire many people after this period but they became increasingly disconnected from the story of his life. His works continued to be copied and studied but fewer and fewer people believed that he would materialize in a second coming to establish a reign of peace and justice on earth.

7

LEGACY

Fazlallah Astarabadi's long-term legacy in the Islamic world corresponds with the ways in which the term Hurufi (Letterist) was understood in the centuries following his death. Some marginal groups put significant stock in his speculations on letters of the Perso-Arabic alphabet and associated themes, although they discounted Fazlallah's messianic claims in favor of their own sociopolitical programs. Such groups saw him as the initiator of a new hermeneutical method that could aid them in exploring esoteric religious mysteries. In total opposition to this appreciative attitude, the mainstream Islamic establishment for the most part came to regard Fazlallah as an arch-heretic whose influence was a sure sign of corruption and sedition. They saw his theories about the alphabet as gibberish that was, besides being meaningless, a severe violation of the sanctity of the Qur'an and other matters central to true Islam.

We can appreciate the fate of Fazlallah's system of thought over the past six centuries by proceeding regionally. In Iran, the movement fully dedicated to his views died out gradually over the fifteenth century but its ideological perspective was assimilated into other movements active on the margins of religion and politics into the modern period. The considerable human as well as ideological traffic from Iran and Central Asia to India in the late medieval period led to some of Fazlallah's ideas finding their way into Indian Islamic thought. Fazlallah's works and the writings of his immediate followers were copied and studied most assiduously in the Ottoman empire, particularly through being adopted by segments of the Bektashi Sufi order. The Bektashis were known for their openness to multiple religious influences and, in the eyes of the mainstream Ottoman establishment, their acceptance of Fazlallah's ideas provided clear proof of their heretical tendencies.

Fazlallah's life story and ideas have held considerable fascination for some modern scholars as well. Here too, some authors have seen his movement as fundamentally subversive, a heresy contrary to central Islamic tenets. Other scholars have emphasized the similarities between the stories of Jesus and Fazlallah, seeing him as a hidden Christ within Islam. Still others have regarded Fazlallah as a proponent of a long-standing tradition of revolutionary esotericism that goes back to pre-Islamic Iran and has always been present in the shadows of mainstream Iranian Islam. Authors inclined to this view highlight Fazlallah's own emphasis on Persian language and ethnicity. Scholars influenced by Marxist historiography have seen Fazlallah and his followers as champions of the downtrodden who were fighting a feudal economic system. For them, Fazlallah's ideology was a precursor to the historical materialism eventually adopted by leftist governments or political parties in the modern era. Finally, Fazlallah's ideas about language and script have been explored in fictional form in the novel *The Black Book* by the prominent Turkish author Orhan Pamuk published in 1990.

IRAN

The second half of the fifteenth century was a highly unstable period in the political history of Iran. Timur's conquests at the end of the fourteenth century had caused severe disruption in civil society. His sons and grandsons who controlled Iran and Central Asia in the first half of the fifteenth century were a fractious group who did not bring the area much stability, although a number of them were great patrons of art and learning in cities like Herat, Samarqand, and Isfahan. The latter part of the fifteenth century saw the rise of Turkic federations named the Qaraqoyunlu (Black Sheep) and the Aqqoyunlu (White Sheep). Some rulers from these federations such as Jihan Shah (d. 1467) and Uzun Hasan (d. 1478) were able to establish solid rule but their states were built around their personal authority, and unraveled rapidly after their deaths. This political instability formed the backdrop for a diverse and lively religious scene with various sects and Sufi orders vying for political patronage as well as adherents.

Although no movement devoted to Fazlallah can be substantiated in Iran after the 1450s, his ideas were not completely forgotten. Manuscripts of his works continued to be copied and the exploration of language and script that he had initiated remained attractive for many people. The last two decades of the fifteenth century saw the rise of the Safavid Sufi order originating from the family of Shaykh Safi al-Din (d. 1334) of Ardabil in Azerbaijan. Leaders of the Safavid family became highly politicized in this period and acquired a large number of Turkic tribal followers who formed a special brotherhood under the name Qizilbash, or Redhead, derived from a special scarlet hat they wore to mark themselves as a distinctive socioreligious group. The Safavid Sufi shaykh and military leader Isma'il (d. 1524) captured the throne of Iran in the first decade of the sixteenth century with the aid of his Qizilbash devotees/soldiers and founded the Safavid dynasty that lasted until 1722.

Shah Isma'il combined the qualities of a capable military and religious leader who inspired great loyalty among his followers. He was not a mere Sufi guide, for the Qizilbash saw him as a materialization of the godhead and the messiah. The place given to Fazlallah and Shah Isma'il in the ideas of their respective followers is quite similar and it is likely that Isma'il was familiar with some of Fazlallah's claims. He wrote poetry in Turkish in the style of the work of Fazlallah's dedicated follower 'Imad al-Din Nesimi and is certain to have encountered Fazlallah's ideas in Nesimi's work. Some verses of doubtful authenticity attributed to him in fact contain praise for Fazlallah and direct references to his doctrines. Isma'il's poetry was, above all, a declaration of his own religious and political claims and he cannot be counted as a follower of Fazlallah. However, he was very likely influenced by some of Fazlallah's ideas in the process of evolving his self-image. He may have encountered them not just in Nesimi, but also in lesser-known individuals active on the Iranian religious scene during the fifteenth century.

A different line of Fazlallah's influence in late medieval Iran can be traced also through Mahmud Pasikhani or Pisikhani (d. 1427), the founder of a movement known as the Nuqtaviyya. Pasikhani was reportedly a student of Fazlallah who broke away from the master because of ideological differences. Instead of letters (*huruf*) he concentrated on the dots (*nuqtas*) that are used to differentiate between consonants in the Perso-Arabic script. Pasikhani also took Fazlallah's theories about the significance of Persian many steps beyond Fazlallah's ideas and saw himself as the prophet of a new Persian-based religion that surpassed Islam. Some scholars connect Pasikhani's religious ideas to Mazdean theories going back to pre-Islamic Iran and see his movement as a revival of a latent Persian religious and cultural identity that had continued to exist in the shadows of the Islamic tradition imposed on Iran following the Arab conquest of Persia in the seventh and eighth centuries. There is little doubt that pre-Islamic Iranian ideas remained influential after the region's Islamization. However, to see the movements that espoused these ideas as a continuous self-conscious "tradition" seems a modern nationalistic view rather than something that can be substantiated from the movements' internal literature. Echoing many of Fazlallah's ideas, works attributed to Pasikhani emphasize the correlation between humanity and divinity and see material reality as the ultimate locus of divine self-manifestation.

The Nuqtavi movement initiated by Pasikhani remained alive in Iran for more than two centuries. In the fifteenth century, it was a part of the spectrum of diverse groups interested in esoteric apocalyptic ideas. This era saw the rise of numerous innovative religious ideologies that both fed off each other and competed for adherents. The Nuqtavis found numerous capable leaders and high profile converts in the Safavid era (1501–1722), though at times they were also subject to severe repression. The Safavid king 'Abbas I (r. 1587–1629) was initiated into Nuqtavi secret doctrines and took the group's prophecies quite seriously. The Nuqtavis in 'Abbas' time predicted that after the first Islamic millennium a Nuqtavi leader would replace the rulers of the day and begin a new Persian cycle. To fulfill this prophecy in a "safe" way, 'Abbas had his Nuqtavi companion Ustad Yusuf Tarkishduz installed as king of Iran on August 5, 1593 (this date falls in the eleventh month of the year 1001 of the Islamic calendar). He was treated as a monarch for three days with 'Abbas himself waiting on him as a courtier. On August 8, Ustad Yusuf was deposed and shot by a firing squad and his body was put on public display. 'Abbas then reclaimed the throne and ordered the arrest and execution of all Nuqtavis in his domain. The movement's political influence declined severely after the staging of this drama but Nuqtavi ideas remained a part of the Iranian intellectual scene.

There is considerable similarity between Fazlallah's ideas and the work of Sayyid Muhammad 'Ali Shirazi (d. 1850), known as the Báb, who instigated a messianic movement in Shi'i Islam and was the precursor to the Baháí religion. While we cannot substantiate a direct link between Fazlallah and the Bab, circumstantial evidence indicates that the two represented the same strain of Iranian Islamic religiosity. This is indicated in their deep mutual interest in cosmogony, cosmology, and esoteric speculation on numbers and the alphabet. Moreover, both of them proclaimed themselves messiahs using complex doctrines emphasizing special knowledge linked to Shi'i and Sufi ideas.

INDIA

Fazlallah's ideas had some influence on Indian Islam through at least two different channels. The Nuqtavi movement traveled from Iran to India as people seeking better fortunes or refuge from persecution moved between these two Persian-speaking Islamic societies in the early modern period. The intellectual circle surrounding the Mughal emperor Akbar (d. 1605) was influenced by Nuqtavi ideas regarding material reality and the supremacy of Persian culture. The Nuqtavis may also have had some effect on Akbar's promulgation of his short-lived Divine Religion (Din-i Ilahi) that was supposed to overcome the differences between existing religions of India.

A quite different strand of Fazlallah's ideology than the Nuqtavi movement is traceable in the literature of the Shattari Sufi order that arrived with a migrating Sufi named Shaykh 'Abdallah Shattar (d. 1485) from Central Asia and became established in India in the late fifteenth and early sixteenth centuries. A detailed comparison between Shattari literature and the literature produced by Fazlallah's movement remains to be undertaken. On a surface level, it is interesting that manuals of spiritual practice produced by Shattari authors contain extensive discussions of the letters of the Arabic alphabet and its symbolic uses. Sometimes by themselves and sometimes in combinations, the letters are seen as the ultimate repositories of the divine names whose characteristics are said to constitute the whole of creation. These ideas, as well as the Shattari emphasis on the *abjad* numerological system, are highly reminiscent of Fazlallah's thought. Shattari works also connect the alphabet to parts of the human body, although here they are substantially influenced by the Indian yoga system that contains an elaborate imagination of the body as a microcosm. No direct link has so far been traced between Fazlallah's works and Shattari literature but the similarity between the two systems is strong enough to suggest at least indirect influence.

THE OTTOMAN EMPIRE

Although Fazlallah's own activity was limited to central Iranian lands, in the long run his works found their most hospitable home in the empire ruled by the Ottoman Turks. The area where Fazlallah had been active during his lifetime was ruled by Turkic dynasties such as the Timurids and the fact that he had followers who were Turks is indicated by the example of the poet Nesimi. The Ottoman dynasty had begun in the late thirteenth century and had suffered the setback of being defeated by Timur in 1402 at Ankara. The Ottomans came back into prominence once again when Timur's empire broke up following his death. They expanded their domains in Anatolia and southeastern Europe in the fifteenth century at the expense of various Turkic Muslim principalities as well as Christian states of Greek and Slavic origins.

Fazlallah's major disciples 'Ali al-A'la and Nesimi both traveled in Anatolia in the first few decades after Fazlallah's death partly because of their appreciation of the region's significance in apocalyptic discourses. As mentioned already, the Muslim messiah, the mahdi, was expected to conquer Constantinople in the course of establishing a kingdom of justice on earth. The movement's effort to recruit the Ottoman prince Mehmet in Edirne circa 1445 before his accession to the throne was symptomatic of a larger propaganda effort in Ottoman lands during the fifteenth century. In 1453, Mehmet did in fact conquer Constantinople, putting an end to the Byzantine empire that the Muslims had seen themselves as called upon to destroy for some eight hundred years. Although Mehmet was fully conscious of the messianic nature of his accomplishment, we have no evidence that he saw himself in the light of Hurufi theories. A century or so later, the Ottoman ruler Süleyman (d. 1566), known as both the Lawmaker and the Magnificent, was portrayed in a messianic role by some court historians, though here as well we have no indication of direct Hurufi influence.

Within Ottoman society, Fazlallah's works received the most hospitable reception in the Bektashi Sufi order. Although named after Hajji Bektash (d. c. 1270) who arrived in Anatolia in the thirteenth century, the Bektashi order became a significant community only in the fifteenth century under the leadership of Balim Sultan (d. 1516). The Bektashis had a somewhat contradictory relationship with the Ottoman state, which was expanding in Anatolia at the same time as the order's own growth. On the one hand, the order became closely associated with the Ottomans' Janissary troops, formed of young boys taken from the empire's Christian subjects and trained for special loyalty to the Sultan. On the other hand, followers of the order were also involved in high-profile rebellions against the Ottomans in Anatolia. The Bektashis also adopted a number of Shi'i ideas in the fifteenth century, as a result of which they were suspected of sympathizing with the Iranian Safavid dynasty that rose to power in the sixteenth century and was one of the Ottomans' most significant rivals. The order combined a number of different ideologies and did not always represent a unified perspective. This internal heterogeneity accounts for the contrary roles undertaken by its adherents over the course of Ottoman history.

The Bektashis traced their connection to Fazlallah through 'Ali al-A'la's Anatolian activities, though there is little historical evidence for direct contact between him and major Bektashi figures. Fazlallah's ideology was likely passed to them indirectly when his works became known in Anatolia following the propaganda carried out by 'Ali al-A'la and others. Whatever the root of the contact, works by Fazlallah and his followers became a special advanced syllabus for Bektashi adepts starting in the fifteenth century. The movement's ideas never became the order's common intellectual currency; they were always deemed a special hermeneutical method learned by the order's sophisticated followers who had already mastered the basic ideology.

Most manuscripts of works by Fazlallah and his followers that survive to the present have Bektashi origins. Long after Fazlallah's original movement had become defunct, the Bektashis kept making copies of them. Fazlallah's narratives read like streams of consciousness with no obvious framework to anchor the reader's comprehension. This meant that, to be understood, they had to be read in conjunction with the works of his followers who had attempted to systemize his ideas in the early part of the fifteenth century. This whole tradition was in Persian, both the standard variety and the Astarabadi dialect, and was added on to by each succeeding generation of scholars interested in the ideas.

The Bektashis for the most part retained the literature in Persian, which also shows that it was accessible only to those who could understand this foreign language in two different dialects. The few notable efforts to render the literature more readily available by translation into Turkish include Abdul Majid Firishteoghlu's (d. 1459–60) précis of Fazlallah's *Book of Eternal Life* (*Javidannama*), entitled '*Ishqnama-yi Ilahi*, and his translations of Fazlallah's *Book of Dreams* (*Khwabnama*) and *The Book of Advice* (*Hidayatnama*). The total amount of literature in Turkish elaborating on Fazlallah's views nevertheless remained very small compared to works copied and studied in the original Persian.

The Bektashi order spread to many corners of the Ottoman empire through its association with the Janissary corps. Adepts of the order took the literature from Fazlallah's movement with them to all these places. This can be seen from numerous surviving manuscripts copied in Egypt, Iraq, Albania, Bosnia, etc. Many Bektashi authors of prose and poetry were deeply affected by Fazlallah's ideas and wrote works in the movement's style. For example, a Bektashi dervish named Gul Baba (d. 1541) popularly known as Misali, who is buried in Budapest, Hungary, authored an extensive compendium of distinctively "Hurufi" ideas entitled *The Key to the Unseen* (*Miftah al-ghayb*). The work of the Bosnian poets Mulhid Vahdati and Husayn Lamekani also shows influence of Hurufi ideas.

As the Ottoman empire underwent large-scale military reforms in the nineteenth century, the Janissary corps lost its privileged status in the empire's machinery. The Bektashi order was banned in 1825 in conjunction with this new policy and its followers took their activities underground. The order's center of gravity shifted from Anatolia and Istanbul to Albania following this repression. Some of the most accomplished modern adepts of Fazlallah's intellectual system have therefore been of Albanian background. John Birge, who studied the Bektashi order in the early twentieth century, found Albanian masters of the order to be avid readers of Fazlallah's works.

Some of Fazlallah's ideas underwent further evolution in the Bektashi environment. A particularly noticeable feature of the Bektashi assimilation of Fazlallah's ideas is a distinctive pictorial art in which letters of the Perso-Arabic alphabet are used to construct forms of human faces and bodies (see Plate 2). Fazlallah's ideas about the lines of hair on the human face and detailed analyses of the shapes of the alphabet and parts of the human body have a pronounced "graphic" bent. However, virtually none of the manuscripts that contain his and his followers' works have any pictorial description of the movement's theories. One can only speculate on this somewhat counterintuitive fact. The movement's ideology always assigned multiple meanings to all texts and other physical realities and it may be that illustrating the material through pictures would have led to an undesirable "reification" of the symbols' meanings. The only special graphic symbols to be found in the movement's manuscripts are the special letter-like characters used to write the name Fazlallah and the numbers twenty-eight and thirty-two (see Plate 1 in Chapter 5). This indicates that the movement's ideologues were quite aware of the power of representing entities in iconic forms. However, they limited their use of this technique to some prominent parts of their ideology.

Bektashi adherents of Fazlallah's system were not bound by the same parameters that seem to have motivated Fazlallah's immediate followers. They took the correspondence between the human body and written text quite literally and fashioned a whole variety of images that located names such as Allah,

Muhammad, ʻAli, Hasan, Husayn, and Fazlallah on the shapes of the human face. These types of Bektashi images do not, for the most part, attempt to illustrate Fazlallah's ideas in pictures.

آدم آن لوح وجود عالمست

فضل حق مسطور وجه آدمست

Plate 2. Bektashi art in which the word *fazl* (grace) forms the features of a human face. The Persian verse underneath the image reads, "Adam is the tablet on which is inscribed the existence of the world/The grace of God (*fazl-i haqq*) is written on Adam's face." From Besim Atalay, *Bektashilik ve Edebiyati* (Istanbul: Matbaʻa-i Amira, 1922).

Instead, they are exemplifications of the general principle of the interchangeability of bodies and texts.

While some Bektashis scoured Fazlallah's works in search of esoteric secrets, his name became indelibly associated with heresy in the mainstream religious establishment of the Ottoman empire. To the degree that they were known, Fazlallah's messianic claim and his ideas about divine incarnation provided ample evidence for this attitude among the empire's Sunni scholars. However, it is noteworthy that the term "Hurufi" was not associated solely with Fazlallah's followers in the Ottoman empire during the fifteenth century. For example, 'Abd al-Rahman al-Bistami (d. 1454), a Sunni author belonging to the normative Hanafi legal school, was known as Hurufi owing to his interest in the esoteric qualities of the alphabet. Bistami was born in Antioch and wrote all his works in Arabic under the patronage of the Ottoman court during the first half of the fifteenth century.

The term Hurufi acquired its negative characteristics in the Ottoman context as Fazlallah became better known particularly through being assimilated in the Bektashi order. From the sixteenth century onward, calling people Hurufi was a standard way for the government and mainstream scholars to brand them as heretics. Historical records provide a number of examples of cases in which individuals were tried for heresy on the charge of being Hurufis, followed by execution. There are quite a few cases of Ottoman Sufis who were not Bektashis but who were still attracted to Fazlallah's ideas. These include mystics and authors belonging to the Mevlevi, Melami, and Hamzevi orders active in Anatolia as well as the Balkan provinces of the Ottoman empire.

Ottoman religious authorities critical of the Bektashi order in the nineteenth century put particular emphasis on Bektashis' positive view of Fazlallah's ideas. A controversy erupted in

Istanbul when Abdul Majid Firishteoghlu's *'Ishqnama*, a fifteenth-century summary of Fazlallah's thought in Turkish, was printed in 1871. A certain Ishaq Efendi roundly condemned the work two years later in a work entitled *The Revealer of Secrets and the Repudiator of the Evildoers* (*Kashif al-asrar ve dafi' al-ashrar*). A Bektashi author named Ahmed Rifat then wrote a refutation of this work three years later, claiming that Hurufi doctrines were separate from the essence of the Bektashi order. The acerbic tone of this literature indicates that association with Fazlallah's ideas was still a highly contentious matter in the nineteenth century. This controversy seems to have subsided in the twentieth century with the general secularization of the public sphere after the creation of the Turkish republic in 1923. Modern Turkish Bektashis or other Sufis seem to show little inclination toward taking Fazlallah's theories seriously.

MODERN INTERPRETATIONS

Cut off from its roots in Sufism and other forms of Islamic esoteric thought, Fazlallah's ideology has also been subject to new interpretation in the modern period. Western scholars such as Clément Huart and E.G. Browne, both writing during the period 1880–1920, investigated Fazlallah's life and works because of their interest in marginal Islamic groups stemming from the Persian environment. These scholars were near contemporaries of the founders of Bábism and Baháism and saw Fazlallah and his followers as an earlier manifestation of the same strand of Persian Islamic esotericism. Helmut Ritter and Hamid Algar, both distinguished scholars of Sufism, have treated the movement in journal and encyclopedia articles. An academic interpretation highlighting the distinctively Persian emphasis of the movement can now be found also in

Kathryn Babayan's book on the cultural landscapes of early modern Iran.

Fazlallah and Nesimi have been championed as early proponents of historical materialism by authors writing in Soviet Azerbaijan. Together with some Iranian leftists active in the 1960s and 1970s, these authors portray Fazlallah and his followers as Iranian or Azeri nationalists who tried to overthrow medieval Islamic civilization in favor of an enlightened "modern" perspective. They are seen as having failed because their time had not yet come, but their ideology is deemed to accord very well with programs proposed or implemented by Marxism-inspired groups active in modern nation-states.

Among modern Muslims, the Turkish scholar Abdülbaki Gölpinarli undertook the most substantial review of Fazlallah's life and thought and the movement's history. Gölpinarli was himself a Mevlevi Sufi with an abiding interest in marginal Sufi groups. He edited some interesting documents relating to the movement's history and his catalogue of manuscripts pertaining to the movement in Turkish libraries published in 1973 is an invaluable tool for anyone wishing to research the topic. Turkish scholars' continuing interest in the topic is reflected in the recent work of Ahmet Yasar Ocak, which has advanced our understanding of Fazlallah's legacy in the larger context of marginal groups active in the Ottoman empire.

ORHAN PAMUK'S *THE BLACK BOOK*

The popular and widely acclaimed Turkish novelist Orhan Pamuk makes use of Fazlallah's life and ideas in his *The Black Book* (*Kara Kitap*) that was first published in 1990 and translated into English in 1994. Pamuk's work exemplifies a postmodernist literary aesthetic and engages numerous topics in the course of weaving a complex and richly allegorical narrative. The plot of the novel centers on a man named Galip whose wife, Rüya, has disappeared without a trace. Galip has been in love with Rüya, who is also his cousin, since childhood and he suspects that she has left him to be with her half brother Jelal who is a famous newspaper columnist in Turkey and with whom she has a close relationship. The chapters of the novel alternate between the perspectives of Galip and Jelal and we are never given a picture of Rüya's own desires or the reasons for her having left Galip.

Pamuk's narrative follows Galip's search for Rüya and Jelal that takes him to all manner of famous and infamous quarters of the city of Istanbul. Galip's pursuit of Rüya mirrors the unending and eventually necessarily fruitless search for the beloved celebrated in the Islamic poetic paradigm. Rüya's silence in the novel fits well with this paradigm as well since the beloved is always talked about endlessly but hardly ever expresses her- or himself in such poetry. The names of the characters in *The Black Book* have historical relevance in that Shaykh Galip (d. 1799) is the name of a famous Ottoman poet and Mevlevi Sufi master who fashioned himself as a successor to the great mystical poet Jalal al-Din Rumi. Rüya literally means dream, and Galip's search for his missing wife in the novel is also clearly a search for his own dreams and identity.

Fazlallah is introduced to the reader in *The Black Book* when Galip stumbles upon the fact that Jelal had been obsessed with his theory about the inherent characteristics of the alphabet. This idea is particularly significant in the Turkish context since the script for writing Turkish was changed from Arabic to Latin letters in the 1920s. Following this transition, Turks are presented as people who have quite literally lost the capacity to read their faces. The language of their bodies is connected to their Ottoman Islamic past inscribed in Arabic letters, while the modern Turkish nation is highly invested in the European-ness represented by the new alphabet based on the Latin script taught in modern schools and universities. The loss of one script and the assimilation of the other represent a change of identity by which subjects are alienated from their true selves. Pamuk illuminates this idea by utilizing Fazlallah's theory that letters are repositories of the highest cosmic truths. As one character in the novel states, modern Turkish identity can become normative only once the faces and bodies of Turks lose their imprints from the old script and become fitted to the molds of the Latin letters.

Pamuk's portrayal of Fazlallah in *The Black Book* is based on standard scholarly treatments of the topic available in the 1980s. His description of Galip's sense of his appreciation of Fazlallah's views is evident in the following passage:

> It gave Galip a feeling of inner peace to read that Fazlallah went from town to town preaching that the world was not a place that yielded up its secrets right off, that it swarmed with secrets, and that in order to penetrate these secrets it was necessary to comprehend the mystery of letters. For Galip, it seemed now to be clearly proved that his world also swarmed with secrets, as he had always anticipated and desired. He sensed that the inner peace he felt was related to the simplicity of this demonstration; if it was true that the world was a place swarming with secrets, then it was also true that the coffee cup on the table, the ashtray, the letter opener, even his own hand that rested like a hesitant crab next to the letter opener, all pointed to and were a part of the existence of a hidden world. Rüya was in this world. Galip was at its threshold. Soon, the secret of letters would let him in (p. 260).

Beyond the basic description, Pamuk's fictional appropriation of Fazlallah's life and the history of the movement veer away from known facts. For example, his descriptions of Hurufis as a vast clandestine network spanning the Ottoman empire have no basis in known facts. However, his literary license allows us the opportunity to appreciate the attraction of Fazlallah's views in a way that cannot be substantiated by purely historiographic methods.

Pamuk's discussion of Fazlallah's ideas also highlights an aspect of the movement that I think was crucial to its attractiveness and partial successes. Fazlallah's worldview was characterized by an intriguing combination of complete certitude and limitless interpretive flexibility. His notion of the metalanguage with its sounds and letters provided the possibility that all of existence could be understood in its essence without any linguistic mediation. A person who knew the metalanguage could both comprehend reality as it truly was and manipulate it because of this power. The human ability to do this was a reflection of the divine creative power; individual human beings who had realized their potential in this regard were full reflections of God himself.

While knowing the metalanguage made a person unambiguously superior to all existent beings, such knowledge could be gathered only through an intense hermeneutical effort directed at all matters apprehended through human mental and sensory faculties. The world was seen as a conglomeration of signs, each one of which had multiple meanings. This perspective opened the world up to limitless interpretation that could become the life's work of anyone committed to the system. Against the distinctly "totalitarian" scope of the theory of the metalanguage, on the practical level, this religious worldview provided unending opportunities for creativity and innovation. Using the myriad of techniques suggested in works by Fazlallah and his followers, one could extract/invent virtually any meaning from phenomena such as texts, shapes of physical objects, geographical data, etc.

Fazlallah Astarabadi was by all accounts a highly charismatic man, but the attraction of his ideas went much beyond the effect of his personality and generated a long intellectual tradition that seems to appeal to people even in the modern secularized world. Perhaps it is his focus on the conjunction between the human body and language – two elements unique to the human species – that accounts for the durability of his vision. His biggest accomplishment lies in that he provided an extensive rationale for the idea that all aspects of existence are interconnected. Once this was established, those inclined to follow him were told to explore all things surrounding them endlessly in intuitive as well as counter-intuitive ways.

Appendix

HURUFI LITERATURE

Fazlallah Astarabadi penned numerous works explaining his religious ideas, most of which are extant in multiple manuscripts. His most extensive work is *The Great Book of Eternal Life* (*Javidannama-yi kabir*), written in the Astarabadi dialect. It runs to more than 800 pages (400 folios) in most manuscripts. Its significance as the ultimate source for Fazlallah's ideology can be gauged from the fact that it survives in multiple copies in Iran and Turkey and can also be found in virtually every major collection of Islamic manuscripts in western Europe. A short account of dreams named *The Book of Sleep* (*Nawmnama*), also in the Astarabadi dialect, is sometimes found in manuscripts of *The Great Book* as an appendix.

Fazlallah's lengthy works in standard Persian include *The Small Book of Eternal Life* (*Javidannama-yi saghir*), *The Book of Love* (*Mahabbatnama*), the narrative poem *The Book of the Divine Throne* (*'Arshnama*), and a collection of verse in the lyric form (*Divan*). All of his narrative works read like rambling streams of consciousness and seem to have no clearly defined internal structure. He moves from topic to topic quite rapidly and is often repetitious. The works are characterized most strongly by reflecting on the text of the Qur'an and, occasionally, the Bible. He was particularly concerned with some Qur'anic passages and ideas, though somewhere or another in his works, he probably had something to say about virtually every verse of the scripture. This is consistent with the fact that he claimed to possess the definitive esoteric interpretation (*ta'vil*) of the text.

The lack of internal organization and consistently idiosyncratic interpretations make Fazlallah's works difficult to decipher. They might be particularly so for a modern reader, though it seems that his original followers also found them difficult to penetrate. If Fazlallah's works are an extended commentary on the Qur'an, the remainder of Hurufi literature is a commentary on his works. This extensive literature is invaluable for making sense of Fazlallah's ideas. Fazlallah's followers were concerned with extracting a consistent religious vision from his inspirations. Their works are much shorter and usually deal with issues in a straightforward way. One difficulty that remains is that much of this literature is in poetry and it is not always possible to decipher the historical references in full. Still, it would be virtually impossible to recover the movement's story and ideology if one could not supplement Fazlallah's works with the movement's subsequent literature.

My reconstruction of Hurufi history and thought has relied on Fazlallah's own writings and numerous later works, many of which are anonymous. This literature is quite vast and even listing the names of the sources here would be too much. Specialist readers interested in the original material are referred to my articles mentioned in Further Reading and the following catalogs and studies:

Azhand, Ya'qub. *Hurufiyya dar tarikh*. Tehran: Nashr-i Nay, 1990.

Browne, E.G. "Further Notes on the Literature of the Hurufi Sect," *Journal of the Royal Asiatic Society* (1907), 533–581.

——. "Some Notes on the Literature and Doctrine of the Hurufi Sect," *Journal of the Royal Asiatic Society* (1898), 61–94.

——. *A Catalogue of the Persian Manuscripts in the Library of the University of Cambridge*. Cambridge: Cambridge University Library, 1896.

Browne, E.G. and Reynold A. Nicholson. *A Descriptive Catalogue of the Oriental Mss. Belonging to the Late E.G. Browne*. Cambridge: Cambridge University Press, 1932.

Gölpinarli, Abdülbâki. *Hurufilik Metinleri Katalogu*. Ankara: Türk Tarih Kurumu Basimevi, 1973.

Huart, Clément. *Textes persans relatifs à la secte des houroûfîs*. Leiden: E.J. Brill, 1909.

Kiya, Sadiq. *Vazhanama-yi Gurgani*. Tehran: Intisharat-i Danishgah, 1951.

Richard, Francis. *Catalogue des manuscrits persans: Ancien fonds*. Paris: Bibliothèque Nationale, Département des Manuscrits, 1989.

Ritter, Helmut. "Studien zur Geschichte der islamischen Frömmigkeit: Die Anfänge der Hurufisekte," *Oriens* 7, no. 1 (June 1954), 1–54.

Rossi, Ettore. *Elenco dei Manoscritti persiani della Biblioteca Vaticana*. Vatican City: Biblioteca Apostolica Vaticana, 1948.

FURTHER READING

Algar, Hamid. "The Hurufi Influence on Bektashism." In *Bektachiyya, Études sur l'ordre mystique des Bektachis et les groupes relevant de Hadji Bektach*, ed. Alexandre Popovic and Gilles Veinstein. Paris: Librairie Orientaliste Paul Geuthner, 1992.

———. "al-A'la, 'Ali," "Astarabadi, Fazlollah," and "Horufism," in *Encyclopaedia Iranica*.

Amanat, Abbas. *Resurrection and Renewal: The Making of the Babi Movement in Iran, 1854–50*. Ithaca: Cornell University Press, 1989.

Amoretti, B. S. "Religion under the Timurids and the Safavids." In *Cambridge History of Iran*, Vol. 6, ed. P. Jackson. Cambridge: Cambridge University Press, 1986.

Babayan, Kathryn. *Mystics, Monarchs and Messiahs: Cultural Landscapes of Early Modern Iran*. Cambridge: Harvard Center for Middle Eastern Studies, 2002.

Bashir, Shahzad. *Messianic Hopes and Mystical Visions: The Nurbakhshiya Between Medieval and Modern Islam*. Columbia, SC: University of South Carolina Press, 2003.

———. "The Alphabetical Body: Hurufi Reflections on Language, Script, and the Human Form." In *Proceedings of the Symposium Religious Texts in Iranian Languages*, ed. Fereydoun Vahman and Claus Pederson. Copenhagen: Det Kongelige Danske Videnskabernes Selskab (forthcoming 2004).

———. "Deciphering the Cosmos from Creation to Apocalypse: The Hurufiyya Movement and Medieval Islamic Esotericism." In *Imagining the End: Visions of Apocalypse from the Ancient Middle East to Contemporary America*, ed. Abbas Amanat and Magnus Bernhardsson. London: I.B.Tauris, 2002.

———. "Enshrining Divinity: The Death and Memorialization of Fazlallah Astarabadi in Hurufi Thought," *Muslim World*, vol. 90, nos. 3 & 4 (Fall 2000): 289–308.

Birge, John Kingsley. *The Bektashi Order of Dervishes*. London: Luzac and Co., 1937.

Burrill, Kathleen R.F. *The Quatrains of Nesimi, Fourteenth-Century Turkic Hurufi*. The Hague: Mouton, 1972.

DeJong, Frederick. "The Iconography of Bektashism: A Survey of Themes and Symbolism in Clerical Costume, Liturgical Objects and Pictorial Art," *Manuscripts of the Middle East* 4, 7–29.

Fleischer, Cornell. "The Lawgiver as Messiah: The Making of the Imperial Image in the Reign of Süleymân." In *Süleyman the Magnificent and His Time: Acts of the Parisian Conference, Galeries Nationales du Grand Palais, 7–10 March, 1990*, ed. Gilles Veinstein. Paris: École des Hautes Études en Sciences Sociales, 1990.

Karamustafa, Ahmet. *God's Unruly Friends: Dervish Groups in the Later Middle Period, 1200–1550*. Salt Lake City: University of Utah Press, 1994.

Norris, H.T. "The Hurufi Legacy of Fadlullah of Astarabad." In *The Legacy of Mediaeval Persian Sufism*, ed. Leonard Lewisohn. London: Khaniqahi Nimatullahi Publications, 1992.

Pamuk, Orhan. *The Black Book*. New York: Farrar, Straus and Giroux, 1994.

INDEX

Note: subheadings are arranged alphabetically, except for those in the entry for Fazlallah, which are arranged chronologically. Page references in *italics* indicate illustrations.

MAKERS *of the* MUSLIM WORLD

Series Editor: Patricia Crone
Institute for Advanced Study, Princeton

Among the over fifty titles in the series:

Ibn 'Arabi
William C. Chittick
Renowned expert William Chittick surveys the life and works of this legendary thinker.
ISBN: 1-85168-387-9

Shaykh Mufid
T. Bayhom-Daou
An assessment of the great Shi'ite scholar and theologian.
ISBN: 1-85168-383-6

Abu Nuwas
Philip Kennedy
A readable introduction to this celebrated 9th-century poet.
ISBN: 1-85168-360-7

'Abd al-Malik
Chase F. Robinson
The Umayyad Caliph and founder of the Dome of the Rock is captured in a concise and clear manner.
ISBN: 1-85168-361-5

Fazlallah Astarabadi and the Hurufis
Shahzad Bashir
Discusses the achievements of this Sufi thinker and founder of Gnostic Hurufism.
ISBN: 1-85168-385-2

al-Ma'mun
Michael Cooperson
An introduction to the controversial 9th-century Caliph and patron of the sciences.
ISBN: 1-85168-386-0

Ahmad Riza Khan
Usha Sanyal
On the founder of the 'Barelwi' movement in India in the late 19th/early 20th centuries.
ISBN: 1-85168-359-3

Amir Khusraw
Sunil Sharma
Surveys the life and work of the 14th-century Indian poet, courtier, musician, and Sufi.
ISBN: 1-85168-362-3

'Abd al-Rahman III
Maribel Fierro
Introduces the founder of the great Caliphate of Madinat al-Zahra at Cordova.
ISBN: 1-85168-384-4

el-Hajj Beshir Agha
Jane Hathaway
An examination of the longest serving Chief Harem Eunuch in the history of the Ottoman Empire.
ISBN: 1-85168-390-9